2013
THE BEST WOMEN'S
STAGE MONOLOGUES

2013
THE BEST WOMEN'S STAGE MONOLOGUES

Edited and with a Foreword
by Lawrence Harbison

MONOLOGUE AUDITION SERIES

SMITH AND KRAUS PUBLISHERS

ISBN: 1575258420/781575258423
ISSN 2329-2709
Library of Congress Control Number:

Typesetting and layout by Elizabeth E. Monteleone
Cover Design: Borderlands Press

A Smith and Kraus book
177 Lyme Road, Hanover, NH 03755
Editorial 603-643-6431 To Order 1-877-668-8680
www.smithandkraus.com

Printed in the United States of America

TABLE OF CONTENTS

FOREWORD

Here you will find a rich and varied selection of monologues for women from plays which were produced and/or published in the 2012-2013 theatrical season. Most are for younger performers (teens through 30s) but there are also some excellent pieces for older women as well. Some are comic (laughs), some are dramatic (generally, no laughs). Some are rather short, some are rather long. All represent the best in contemporary playwriting.

Several of the monologues are by playwrights whose work may be familiar to you, such as Don Nigro, Theresa Rebeck, David Mamet, Nilo Cruz, David Ives and Christopher Durang; others are by exciting up-and-comers such as Nicole Pandolfo, Adam Cunningham, Greg Pierce, Colman Domingo, Sharon Goldner, Begonya Plaza, Paul Downs Colaizzo and Greg Kalleres.

Many of the plays from which these monologues have been culled have been published and, hence, are readily available either from the publisher/licensor or from a theatrical book store such as the Drama Book Shop in New York. A few plays may not be published for a while, in which case contact the author or his agent to request a copy of the entire text of the play which contains the monologue which suits your fancy. Information on publishers/rights holders may be found in the Rights & Permissions section in the back of this anthology.

Break a leg in that audition! Knock 'em dead in class!

Lawrence Harbison
Brooklyn, NY

MONOLOGUES

Seriocomic
Maria, Twenties

Maria is talking to Tommy, the bartender in a joint in New Jersey, with whom she has had sex with the night before, about her former fiancée, Danny, who died tragically in a fall.

MARIA: Don't remind me about Danny. I just . . . don't understand people. Like, why do they pretend one thing with you, only to need something totally different? Anyway, I'd rather be alone, really. It's so much easier.
  (a beat)
Do you ever feel like . . . like I don't know. That you missed something that was important? Like on the way you choose left instead of right and missed the way you were supposed to go. Like somehow you accidentally fucked it all up? But you can't figure out how or where or when it went wrong?
  (a beat)
Fucking cigarettes. I just had to go get cigarettes.
  (a long pause)
If I hadn't left, maybe we would have went inside. I would have sat on his lap and had another glass of champagne. Maybe we would have went into the bathroom to fuck. We used to like to do that. Have sex in people's bathrooms during parties. I don't know why. We weren't like that, like spontaneous, in any other circumstance, but we liked to fuck in people's bathrooms during parties.
  (a pause)
We would have gotten married last week. If it hadn't, you know if he wasn't dead. Right when I got my ticket to Newark. I was packing my bags to come home about

when I would have been packing them to go on my honeymoon. And get this. We were gonna go to Vegas. And get married again by Elvis. We both really wanted to do that—to get married by Elvis, but his mom had a fit and wanted it to be a Catholic wedding—but we both really wanted Elvis. So we were gonna do it. Do both. Catholic wedding in New York and then a honeymoon in Vegas.

(a beat)

I just love Elvis. And what's fucked up about life. Fate. The Stars. Whateverthefuck is ruling this goddamn circus—is that I was in Vegas. I went to Vegas. Only there was no Elvis. And no Bobby. But I was there just when I was supposed to be. Somehow. Do you think I'll ever feel better?

Information on this playwright may be found at:
www.smithandkraus.com.
Click on the AUTHORS tab.

Comic

Beth, Forty-two

Beth Slattery is a former cheerleader and the wife and mother at the center of the play. Beth has just arrived home after making her first big sale at a new real estate job and recounts her day to her husband, Mike, an NFL football player. She's spent the last sixteen years of her life as a full time wife to her NFL football player husband and mom to her teenage twins, so having success on her own is exhilarating. Mike—who was once the star of the family but is now retired and searching—has just told his kids that he's planning to ask Beth for a divorce. He tries to tell her, but Beth is so excited she doesn't give him a chance.

BETH: I sold the Ocean Parkway house! The motherfucking bigass loaded mansion, baby! With the motherfucking four hundred THOUSAND dollar commission. I knew it. I knew I was good at this. DAMN, it feels good to be good at something. I'm a breadwinner! I'm winning bread! God, I feel so amazing right now. I want a drink. Want a drink? We should have a drink. We should toast. What did you guys get? I know, I know. I'm sorry. I'm sorry I didn't call. My boss took me out and—you know, you want them to think you don't have a life and you don't have kids and there's nothing you'd rather do than work 24/7 and when you're done working a twelve hour day, oh, you'd like to go out for DRINKS but man oh MAN my boss was happy. And the best part is, this is just the beginning. I'm gonna get bigger and bigger listings now, it's what happens, you get one big sale and then they all just topple like DOMINOS. God, I have spent the last twenty YEARS feeling worthless and like such a WASTE of space and finally I feel like I accomplished something. It feels. SO. Good. Do you want to have sex? I really want to have sex. Does it turn you on that I'm a fucking champion? Let's fuck all night, okay? Let's just fuck all night and then we'll drink some Gatorade and then we'll fuck some more.

Information on this playwright may be found at:
www.smithandkraus.com.
Click on the AUTHORS tab.

Dramatic
Jakey, Thirties

Jakey is speaking to a wealthy owner of the Ohio racetrack that employs her. She cares about him but she recently claimed/purchased/took a horse away from him because he was running the horse as a two year old, which can be damaging. 1960's.

JAKEY: I ain't talkin' about the horse. Robert, a racetrack is a place where the workers work but are too poor to own what they are workin' for. And the owners own what they don't work for or deserve or understand. You ever had your arm up a horses ass clear to your shoulder? Ever slept in a stall to keep a horse from havin' nightmares and shattering his knees on the stable wall? I get up at four every mornin' to be at the track by five and most of my crew is already there. They see the sun come up and go down from the shed row and on Friday night they cash a paycheck for two hundred dollars and they feel rich till Saturday morning. And eventually we pass the animal on to you. That horse goes zero-to-forty in three strides, and everyone heralds you as a truly savvy horseman. And now that the horse is dirty, exhausted, weak and done in, you pass the reigns back to the two-hundred-dollar-a-weeker who stays up all night tryin' to heal the animal from the days abuse. And sure, you can say it's a job like any other. Your chauffer takes care of your car and the harbormaster takes care of your boat. But this is a livin' breathin' animal that gets loved and nurtured then abandoned to strangers for money. And that's damage. To me, to the horse, to everyone. And especially to you, Robert, 'cause you never really know what it's like to be part of something, to actually be in the heart of the race.

Comic
Amber, early Twenties

After having sex with Cecil Ravinsdale, the host of the TV talent competition America's Brightest Star, Amber asks Cecil to rank her performance. He does, and it's not kind. After he finishes his harsh critique which nearly leaves her in tears, Amber strikes back.

AMBER: You have a small penis. You do. It is below average. What was that, four inches while hard? And not very thick. If you're going to be four inches, at least give me a little something to work with, so I feel something. I may be young, but I have seen seven penises so far . . . well, eight now, and you know where you rank? Seventh. John Baker had a smaller penis, but the only time I was with him he sort of came really quickly while he was semi-hard, so I'm not really sure. You could be the smallest. No wonder you put your underwear back on right away. To hide the evidence. Which was already pretty well hidden. And what's with the grunting? More like a squeal. I'm not trying to be rude, but you sounded like my little brother's guinea pig when it was hungry and begging for food. What kind of man sounds like that? And you don't smell very good. I don't care if it's Jordan by Michael Jordan. It stinks. And your balls stink. Maybe I would have blown you for longer if you smelled a little better. On a scale of 1 to 10, 10 being Ryan Gosling and 1 being Jeff Horkins, who is my brother's idiot friend, I'd give you negative eight million. You definitely rank eighth out of eight. And I can't wait to tell my viewers. Good day, sir.

Comic
Amber, early twenties

*Amber records her latest entry in her VLOG, a video diary
she uploads to the internet. In previous VLOG entries she
talks about her plan to move to Hollywood and become a
famous celebrity. This is her first entry after making the
arrangements to make it to Hollywood.*

AMBER: I have some very exciting news. So, Mr. Producer
man . . . well, he begged to see me, and guess what?
(She beats out a drumroll on her leg.)
He's taking me to Hollywood! Yep, the big city and me!
The next time I film this VLOG, I'll be coming to you
from my glamorous new digs in sunny Southern Cali-
fornia. This week will be my last here in this town, so
don't panic if I go a few weeks without updating. I won't
be staying with him, of course, but I'm sure his guest
house will do nicely. I couldn't have done it without all
your help. I want you all to know that you are my closest
friends, and I cherish all the time I've spent talking to
you, and reading your responses. Your support has been
wonderful, and it's on the strength of your backs that has
enabled me to stand so tall. I'd also like to thank my agent
and everyone at the studio, who were all very helpful in
getting my career going. Let's see, all my wonderful co-
stars, who made me look better every day. Of course, I
made them look great from day one! Oh, I had so many
more people to thank, but now that I'm actually up here,
I don't really remember everything! Ugh . . . my acting coach would kill me for blanking. I must thank the
loves of my life, of course, my dogs Bipsy and Nipsy.
Boys, mama's bringing you steak tomorrow! And lastly,

I know, the music is kicking in, but just give me a few more seconds please, thanks . . . And lastly, all of you, because if none of you had watched me, if none of you had tuned into my early days of having a VLOG, then I wouldn't exist. Without you, I don't exist.

THE ASK
David Lee White

Comic
Sally, mid-twenties to mid-thirties

Sally has just joined the board of her local theatre and has taken Darren out to dinner in order to ask him for a $10,000 contribution. She is completely unaware that Darren's wife has recently died. After Sally makes "the ask," Darren tells her that he thought they were on a date. Humiliated, Sally tries to turn the situation around and begins seducing Darren by telling him how much she loves the theatre.

SALLY: I want this. I mean maybe I want this. Actually, for sure, I am definitely, maybe ready for a relationship. I mean we've got some differences to overcome, sure. We're from different worlds and all that. I'm a simple girl that lives within my means, you know? And you're an extra special rich guy with golf clubs and snow-globe doorknobs and Monet paintings in the bathroom. But you gotta know something about me. Sometimes, I'm fucking crazy. Like really emotionally needy, like cry-for-no-reason crazy. But—BUT—it's only because I'm so full of passion! And here's something you gotta know about me. I mean if we're gonna be together, this is something you have to learn to embrace. I love art. Love it. Look at me in fucking eyes and you'll be able to see how serious I am. Serious like cancer. Sorry. A heart attack. I love everything about art. And you know what the best art is? Theatre. I love the way it makes me feel. I love the way it frees my mind. I love the way it breaks down the walls of convention and makes us ask questions that we never dared to ask. I love the messed up red chairs that hurt my ass and the pretentious production photos in the lobby. I love the stupid sweatshirts and the over-priced

Shakespeare paperbacks in the gift shop. But most of all, I love the people that make theatre. I love how they cuss in front of each other in the workplace like it's something to be proud of. I love how the actors flirt with each other and give one another unnecessary backrubs. I love how they can go from laughing to crying in about two seconds and mean absolutely every bit of it. I love how they eat nothing but couscous but still manage to smoke enough cigarettes to choke a pack-mule. I love how they blame everyone else for the fact that they don't make enough money. I love how the directors scream and insult everyone they meet so they can sound smarter and more passionate than the rest of us. I love the theatre technicians that absolutely refuse to do anything productive until they've bitched for it for at least an hour. I love that. My God, I more than just love those people. I want to be those people. I want to live my life on the edge. I want to have sex that I only barely remember. I want to argue about politics and pretend that I watch the news. I want to complain that there's no cot in the dressing room. I want to be difficult and cranky and have bags under my eyes and a constant, small, hacking cough that spreads through the entire cast until it becomes pneumonia. So are you ready Darren? Are you ready to take that leap with me? Are you ready to be on that fucked up roller-coaster for the rest of your life?

Information on this playwright may be found at:
www.smithandkraus.com.
Click on the AUTHORS tab.

Dramatic
Cathy, early sixties

As a young woman, Cathy was a member of a radical group. During a bank robbery, she shot and killed two police officers. She has been incarcerated for 35 years, during which time she has become a born-again Christian. She has a parole hearing coming up and hopes to persuade her parole officer, Ann, to recommend her release.

CATHY: Don't you see? You are chained to the past.
  When you can be free.
  This is the lesson of The Christ. To let the
  dead bury the dead. That is all that it means,
  Ann, to be reborn. It is not "mystical" that
  you need be frightened of it.
  It is not an "ordeal" it is a gift.
    (pause)
  Of which you've dreamed. The end of regret.
  "The People . . . were moved by Christ's word.
  For I do not think that they were
  swayed by Magnetism. But by logic.
  Which, however abstruse can only rest
  upon assumptions, which is to say, upon Faith.
  All act on Faith. The saint and
  the criminal, whose faith is that there
  is no Judgment. This is the sin against
  the Holy Ghost,"
  that Spirit which unites the Father
  and the Son. It is a mystery. Which is
  the essence of Faith. Ann: neither
  God nor human worth can be proved. That,
  finally, there is nothing but Spirit.

In time. I could by Reason, Ann, bring you to
Faith. I know your heart is heavy.
Because it is stone. Which must break to
be opened. Will you break open your heart?
You can lay your burden down.
And He will take it from you.
I can't do it for you, Ann.
I wish I could. He can.

Seriocomic
Mary, a young prostitute, nineteen

Mary Patterson, a beautiful young prostitute on the streets of Edinburgh in the late 1820's, is in love with a young doctor who works for a famous Anatomist, dissecting corpses. The young doctor loves her but is reluctant to rescue her from her career on the streets, in fear of ruining his career. She is bitter and angry, and hurt, but here she tries to drown her hopes of marriage and a normal life and see her profession as empowering.

MARY: Getting hurt is just life. I don't care. I'm a strong girl. At worst, I'll end up the best old whore in Edinburgh. I'm not going to worry about men any more, ever. Drown all the babies and rake in the money. Then when I get to Heaven, I'll have enough cash to bribe my way in. And then no more relations with Mary Patterson. A palace in Heaven and no more relations. I've seen the light now, Janet. Maybe I did let myself believe a fellow loved me, but it's all clear now. I won't be foolish any more about it. The way I see it, there's no harm in whoring. The body is just a big, smelly thing the soul is trapped in. And Lord knows, we can't profit off the beauty of our bodies very long, so we might as well make the most of it while it's still a money-maker. Beauty doesn't last. Joy doesn't last. Liquor doesn't last. Not that I wouldn't get out of it if I could. But then I think, what's the difference? We're all whores of one sort or another. A certain young man I know would have us believe we're just a heap of guts inside and no more than that. The body's just something to be used. And everybody does. He uses it. Why shouldn't I make a living off it? If you don't own your own body, what do you own? And if you can't make a living off your own flesh, what have you got? The sons of bitches have taken everything else from us. Do they want to own our bodies and our souls both?

Information on this playwright may be found at:
www.smithandkraus.com.
Click on the AUTHORS tab.

Seriocomic
Mary, a young prostitute, nineteen

Edinburgh, Scotland, in the late 1820s. Mary Patterson, a beautiful young prostitute, in despair over her rejection by a young doctor who loves her but can't risk destroying his career by marrying her, has allowed herself to be lured to the lodgings of Burke and Hare, who are in the business of murdering the poor and selling their corpses to Dr. Knox's anatomy class for dissection. It's late at night, Mary's been given enough liquor to lower her suspicions, and now she is getting into bed, believing that all her companion, the sullen giant Hare, wants from her is copulation. In fact, when she is asleep, he will strangle her so he can sell her body to the anatomist. These are her last living moments.

MARY: Well, then, I suppose I'd better start earning my keep, if I'm going to stay. I don't want anybody saying Mary Patterson didn't earn her keep. Lord, it's cold tonight. Under the covers we go. This is not such a terrible bed, considering some of the places I've slept. It's better than huddling under trash bins in the alley. On a cold night like this, sometimes I just want to curl up in a warm bed and never wake up. Or wake up in Heaven. Or sleep a thousand years, and wake up someplace where it's warm. It's never warm enough in Edinburgh, at least not for me, except when it's too hot. You'd better get me while you can, Mr Hare, for I'm drifting off fast. Unless you like your women to be snoring. Don't be shy, Mr Hare. Are you shy? You're a big, strong, fellow, aren't you? I must warn you that I have bad dreams, too. I dream about the filthy streets and alleys that I wander in. Dirty places, horrible dreams. In my dreams, I'm lost, and can't be found. And then I wake up, and I haven't been dreaming at all. I wonder what the Queen of France dreams about. Do you know what I'd do, if I was the Queen of France? First, I'd kill the King. Then I'd kill all the doctors. We'd all live a good deal longer if there were no doctors. They feed on death. Like ghouls. Doctors are ghouls. Do you think we get to keep our bodies in Heaven, Mr Hare? Because I don't think I want mine. Although other people might. I'm told it's quite a nice body, and sometimes I am fond of it, looking in shop windows at it, but I think I'd rather just be a breath of air. Just a mouthful of air on a June morning is all I'd like to be. Just a mouthful of air.

Information on this playwright may be found at:
www.smithandkraus.com.
Click on the AUTHORS tab.

Dramatic
Norma, twenty-five to forty

Norma, a social worker who works with the mentally ill, is bringing patients their morning medications. As the play begins, she addresses the audience.

NORMA: What the hell was I thinking? I wanted to get out of my depression. So I came to work in a mental ward. That's like trying to get rid of your fever by crawling into an oven. The people here fill up their days with little art projects and inane chores the doctors assign them. Jon checks the other patients for head lice. Jackie buffs the floor with a sock. All day. Every day. But the most pathetic thing is Jon and Jackie got this idea they're married. They can hardly have a ten second conversation without one of them going into convulsions. And now it looks like Jon's sleeping around. He's not in his bed or hers. When Jackie finds out they'll need to bring out the restraints and give her a half dozen injections. Too bad I won't be in on the fun. After this shift I'm out of here. Freedom. My life has been transformed by a tooth paste commercial. This woman in the ad is invincible because of her smile. All around her guys fall off ladders but she just walks right through. Blue silk scarf fluttering in the breeze. Toothy smile sparkling in the sun. In my desperate state the image seemed profound. So I did like the toothpaste woman. Put a bounce in my step. Bought a dozen blue silk scarves. And started smiling. Constantly. When people asked how I was instead of describing my depression I smiled. Then they smiled. Soon I was surrounded by a bunch of smiling people. But when the smiling people asked about my work, then what. Didn't want to say I provide inadequate assistance to people with terrible illnesses for a degrading salary. So I said I'm applying for a fancy bank job. I applied for one. And I got it. I'll have clients. Assistants who treat me like a grownup. And a love life. Guy saw me smiling like an idiot. Couldn't resist. He's totally different from other guys I've been with. He's sane. It's a stretch for me, I know. But it's been such a long dry spell I'm willing to overlook the fact that he's reliable and fun to be with. He's picking me up this afternoon and taking me to his place upstate for the weekend. Would have been nice to have made a dent here. Cured people. Ended human suffering as glorious music poured down from the sky. But I'm getting myself out of bed in the morning. A miracle in its own right.

Dramatic
Crystal, late twenties

Crystal is a saleswoman at a Saturn dealership. She is speaking to a recalcitrant, slightly odd customer who may or may not want to buy a car. Crystal really needs to close the deal, as she is practically destitute.

CRYSTAL: What our customers have found is that the places that say they negotiate are really just jacking up the price to begin with, so that's the great thing about Saturn: total price transparency. We put it all right there on a sheet of paper. I might be able to throw in some free Saturn merchandise. But if buying American is something that doesn't matter to you then I don't know what else I can say. If you want to buy something that came from a factory in Oki-saka-whatever, then go right ahead. But when you buy a Saturn you're buying American ingenuity and American jobs; from the person who hands you the keys all the way back to the guys on the line in Spring Hill, Tennessee; it's like a family. And when you buy a Saturn, you can feel yourself becoming a part of that family. Charlie, I don't think you're really undecided. I think you know exactly what you want to do. I've told you about the features of this car until I'm blue in the face. So you want to know how this car is going to change your life. Oh, Charlie. You've hit on the exact reason why I love selling cars. Because other than a house, I think a car is the single most life-enhancing purchase a person can make. Your car is like a second skin. You're in it every day. You live in it, you escape in it, you can even sleep in it . . . I've done that. If you have a family, it can change your relationship with your kids. If you're a single guy, it can be the thing that gets you laid. It's the face you show the world. It's you.

Dramatic
Ida, eighteen, African American

Ida is talking to her boyfriend Wynn about the four-building housing project where she lives.

IDA: Fucking neighborhood stinks in the summer. All this heat. Don't matter anyway. Everybody sees everything, but they don't care. Everybody is always out, in the streets. Day and night. People on stoops, leaning on cars, hanging out of windows. You can't get away from nobody. Building 1 . . .
  [Ida turns in the direction of the first building]
. . . see? There's Mr. Wheeler smoking up, reading the paper. Building 3
  [turns in the direction of the third building]
Sasha is on the phone running her mouth. Building 4
  [turns]:
Mrs. James is greasing her scalp. Building 2
  [turns]:
my mama is sitting up there sleeping. Four buildings make up this project. And every building got seven floors. And every floor got 11 windows going across it. All those windows facing down to this courtyard, those benches. So Mr. Wheeler was smoking. So Sasha was talking bullshit. Mrs. James was sitting by the window, listening to the radio. But nobody said nothing to me. Nobody asked me anything. Am I crazy? I don't know if I'm crazy. Don't know if I'm making shit up. Am I cracking out? Sitting up in my dingy ass apartment, hiding out from what? From who? Something I made up? Must've. Had to have made it up cause nobody said nothing. It wasn't nothing. Nothing for me to sprint pass these benches every day.

This is the only way out to the street, Wynn. When I leave my building I have to cross through here to get to the street. Every other exit is blocked by a fence with a thick chain and fat padlock keeping it shut. I can't even choose how I come and go. I'm glad I met you downtown at a movie theater. Nowhere near here cause otherwise I'd only see all this *[re the projects]* when I look at you. But I don't. I don't, Wynn. And that's why I like you. That's why I need you.
   (Pause)
I'm going home. I'll talk to you later.

BLACKTOP SKY
Christina Anderson

Dramatic

Ida, eighteen, African American

Ida is talking to Klass, a young man who lives on a bench in the projects where she lives, about a demonstration she has just been to.

IDA: !! Justice for our Streets !!
!! Justice means Peace !!

Klass, oh my god, Klass you shoulda seen it! People everywhere! Signs everywhere! Speeches! Chants! Shit, I should protest more often. I feel good!! You should start one. You should make a sign then go down and call out those ignorant muthafucks sittin in those big offices. Shame those ignorant money whores who are only interested in helping A people not THE people, you know? They only interested in a certain kind of people who don't LOOK nothin like me or you. Who don't LIVE like me or you. ESPECIALLY you. Go down there and bust some knowledge in the face of those dudes who makin your life so hard. Got you out here livin like this. We need to get you down there, Klass. But, but you need a chant though. We need to write a good one for you. You gotta yell something in repetition. Make it have a rhythm to it. Not too many words. Gotta be simple and to the point. So those cash hoes know what you saying. They gotta know what you're willing to do for your rights. For your justice. It's gotta be short cause the more you say your chant, the more you believe it. You start yelling it. Getting loud!! And you feel it coming from your toes, your nose, your, your lips, your eyeballs:

!! Justice for our Streets !!
!! Justice means Peace !!

This is how it's going down: I'll make signs. One for me. One for you. And t-shirts. We can make those together. We'll make t-shirts. These *[re: the one she's wearing]* cost 10 bucks or some shit. We'll make some t-shirts. We'll go in the streets and keep marching and chanting 'til they right the wrongs!

Comic
Jeanine, twenties

*Jeanine has just discovered a baby (Bob) in the bathroom
of the restaurant where she works and has fallen in love
with him and taken him. While driving, she tries to explain
her reasons why.*

JEANINE: I was finishing up my Sunday night dinner at the
Bamboo Wok. I don't know how authentic or healthy it is
but I like the flavors. I'd been working my way through
the menu for about a year. Each week, I would have a
new entrée in order of appearance. I'd finally made it to
the "Noodles slash Rice" section after several months
of Lamb and I felt like I was entering a new era in my
life. When the waiter delivered the check and cookie,
the fortune inside seemed different. The paper looked
shiny, almost golden, the ink darker, more insistent. "You
will be the mother to a great great man." The fortunes
I usually get are a little more vague than that. But this
felt intentional. Like someone was watching me. From
inside the cookie. It made me smile. I thought "well,
cool, Jeanine, maybe the future isn't only selling tiny
burgers and having Asian food once a week." And then
my stomach started to twitch, felt like I was gonna be
sick. I started sweating, breathing heavy. And I thought
Oh my god, it's happening already. I stood up from my
table and shouted "I'm gonna be the mother to a great
great man!" Next thing I knew I woke up in a hospital
bed. At first I thought I'd conceived my great man im-
maculate till the nurse told me that I'd almost died at the
restaurant. That I had a severe reaction to the gluten in
Asian noodles slash rice that messed up my insides so
much that I would never be able to make a "Great Great

Man" the regular way. I don't really care for fortunes very much anymore. But, funny, you know, there you are. There you are. I will give you food and shelter. I will educate you. I will make sure that becoming President of the United States remains a possibility. Even if it kills me, I will make you a great great man.

Comic
Nikki, twenties to thirties

Nikki is in a bar with her friend Tiffany. Tiffany has asked Nikki how many times she has gone out with a guy Nikki has recently started dating. Nikki has found a woman's shoe in the guy's apartment.

NIKKI: Tom acted really weird when I brought up the future of our relationship and we've already been out three times!! Plus four phone conversations—one that was like 55 minutes—so really, we've been out 4.6 times and we've had sex twice—both on date three, which, as I said, was really date 4.6 so it's not like I'm a slut and we had a real connection but now I don't know what to think! I thought he lived alone; although he is a teacher and he probably doesn't make that much money so maybe he has a roommate—but he never mentioned one and I know he's got a daughter but she lives with her Mom and I don't think this was his weekend unless maybe they switched weekends, but I think she's like ten and this is not the shoe of a ten year old. Maybe his daughter was there and his ex came to pick her up and she lost the shoe but what, then she just left with one shoe? Like, you'd notice something like that right? It's not an earring. Those, sure, they get lost without you noticing, but a shoe? No one loses a shoe and doesn't know it unless they're totally stoned. Oh My God, what if his ex was there and she was totally stoned—what if they were both high? It's like a aphrodisiac after all and what if they—OH MY GOD! Is this his ex's shoe? Would he tell me? Was she there? Are they TOGETHER? Or is it something else entirely?!

Information on this playwright may be found at:
www.smithandkraus.com.
Click on the AUTHORS tab.

Dramatic
Pat, forty

It's 1952, and Richard Nixon is about to go on national television to explain to the American people about the "slush fund" he has been accused of having. Nixon is perilously close to being dumped from the ticket by Eisenhower and the party bosses. His initial impulse is to lash out angrily, attacking his critics. His wife Pat here urges him to focus on his better side—the side that made her fall in love with him.

PAT: Do you know what story the girls love for me to tell them? The story of our courtship. You know what they love? They love when I tell them how I wouldn't give you the time of day when you first asked me out. They make me tell it every bedtime. I say, "I wouldn't give Daddy the time of day" and Julie says, "So what did Daddy do?" And I tell them, "Well, he just wouldn't give up." They love that. And they love when you asked me to the dance and I said I had a date—Anyway, even though I've told them a hundred times about the date with Teddy, they always say, "Tell us what Daddy did when you said no," so I say, "Well, neither Teddy nor I had a car and so Daddy drove me to Teddy's house and then drove us both to the dance." The first time I told them this, Julie said, "How embarrassing for Daddy!" but I explained to her that you were outsmarting me. You knew that during that long drive to Teddy's house I'd get to know you better. And the better I knew you the more I'd like you. When I tell them that you waited for me, for hours, to drive me home after the dance, Tricia always says, "That's love!" You know what else it is?

It's a kind of bigness of spirit. That's what I love about you, Dick, that you're—that deep down you won't give up if you know something is right and that what's right is so—big. You bet on yourself—that if you swallowed your pride and drove me, I'd make the right choice. And look what we have because of it, our beautiful family. And sometimes people don't see that side of you, my side because sometimes you focus on—what didn't go your way. But don't you think I've had my heartbreaks? I've felt cheated, too, just the way you have but I try to smile and push on—Don't you think I felt cheated when Mom died? *I was 12.* Even before she died but once the cancer, you know, really had a hold of her, I had to take her place in the house. I made every meal for Dad and my brothers, I did their laundry, cleaned the house—and I had to keep up with my school work. I can remember propping my vocabulary book up on the ironing board while I did the pleats in my school uniform. Artesia didn't have a hospital, so Mom's doctor charged us three dollars a week and he kept her in a room at his house. It sounds so small now but, my God, back then that three dollars was—such a strain. And every night after dinner, I'd walk over to Dr. Penn's house and I'd read to her or help her with whatever she needed, you know, like changing her nightie or just making her pillow nice again.

(ruefully)
I thought if I made her comfortable, it would make the cancer go away. As I said, I was 12. It seemed like she stayed in that house forever. Sometimes, hope makes things seem longer. But it was only three weeks until she—

(She pauses, afraid she might lose her composure. Regroups. Proceeds kindly but firmly:)
Anyway, you didn't get into the club you wanted. I'm sorry. You couldn't afford to go to the college you wanted. Neither could I. Everybody gets cheated. FDR had polio for God's sake. Our losses only mean something to us. Nobody else wants to hear about them—Because *they*

Lawrence Harbison

have their own. Polio, Dick, he had polio, and he never stopped smiling. So all I want to say about your speech is: write your best self. No anger, no 'they-didn't-give me-this,' or 'they-kept-me-out-of-that.' Let them see the you that our girls loved to hear about, and everything will go our way.

.

Comic
Sonia, forty

*In this direct address to the audience which starts the play,
Sonia talks about how she has just turned forty. She's not
happy about it.*

The sound of a fart.

SONIA: What?
   (to audience)
That wasn't me OKAY.
   (beat)
What? You think I'm gassy cuz I ate a chimichanga?
Huh? Maybe its because, lately, vodka tastes like tap
water AND my eyes look like a third world country.
OH and smiling, just seems obsolete my heart feels like
a metal weight in my chest Affecting the gravitational
pull of my insides AND voices of people that died seem
to ring in my ears. Like an old teacher of mine, who once
told me "Sonia, youth is walking down a hallway with
hundreds of open doors, and as you get older and time
passes doors close and close . . ." AND fast forward to
this morning, I woke up BLOATED after my 40th birthday dinner cuz I went a little loco and had four chimi-
fucking-changas. I looked past my panza to see a pair
breasts that USED to look ambitious on my chest AND
rolled over to a man that has these gross grey HAIRS
growing out of his ears, AND fumbled into my closet to
find that my daughter gave me a pair of PANTUFLAS
for my birthday! FUCKING PANTUFLAS, I'm 40 not
65 damn it. This can't really be how my life turned out,
right? If met the 20 year old version of myself NOW I
think she would kick me in the Cho Cho, so that I could

feel SOMETHING, ANYTHING again. I mean, I'm 40 years old, damn it. I want to say that with an excited inflection in my voice, not the pouty tone that mimics my breasts. AND, I FUCKING hate being bloated. None of my pants fit!

Information on this playwright may be found at:
www.smithandkraus.com.
Click on the AUTHORS tab.

Comic
Sonia, forty

Sonia has left her husband and daughter to go off and find herself again. In this direct address to the audience, she talks about how Zoloft is making her feel better.

SONIA: The first time I took anti depressants, I felt so . . . Defeated? Is that the right word? There I was, this woman with wrinkles on my knuckles and thick veins infesting the back of my hands, like my mothers. Pesky grey hairs on my head and memory slipping from my brain like water running through my finger tips. Here I was this GROWN woman sitting calmly at the kitchen table with a tall glass of water and a small green pill grinning up at me from the table. Zoloft is like pot, seriously, its green and makes your eyes squinty from mass stimulation, your heart delirious and your stomach opinionated. I wondered if my shrink had ever taken Zoloft, or smoked weed or felt the type of thick depression that chronically fogged up my life. I must have sat there for a good hour, just staring at that pill and thinking about my mother, the way her eyes were always swollen as if she had always been crying. My last thought was Ricardo, well the sound he makes when he is frustrated with my moods. It's an interesting mix between a scoff and a gargle from his throat. Like an "URGGGGHH." I've been putting up with your bullshit for 16 years bitch "uggggggh". I took that stupid little green pill and shoved it down my throat like it was zuchinni, and I HATE zucchini but I read on the internet that is really good for your eyes. And well, I want to be able to see better. Just see, especially what's right in front of me.

Information on this playwright may be found at:
www.smithandkraus.com.
Click on the AUTHORS tab.

CONEY
David Johnston

Dramatic
Shelley, thirties

SHELLEY is a lesbian in her thirties. The place is Coney Island, the present day. She sits on a bench speaking to MARNI, a teenaged girl who is not getting along with her father, whom she has just met.

SHELLEY: That's the thing about "The Warriors." They're trying to get back to the sea. They live in Coney. The ocean is where they draw their strength. When they go up to the Bronx, they're cut off. The sea is their strength. That's why they have to get back to it. While they're by the sea, nothing can hurt them. It's their turf. All those other gangs. The guy with the bottles on his fingers. None of that can hurt them anymore. They've found their strength. That's what happened to me. What happened to me is like when "The Warriors" went to the gang conference in the Bronx. I left the sea. I cut myself off from my strength. I lost who I am. I moved to Park Slope. And I love her. I love my girl. She wants to live in the Slope. She doesn't like Coney. She says it's gross. I tell her it's getting better, you'll like it. But no. She wants to be near dykes. Dyke bars. Dyke coffee shops. Dyke herbs. Places that sell soymilk. Rice milk. Every kind of milk except—milk. And I love her. I love the smell of her and her taste and how she looks in the morning and I just fucking love her. And that's something about me, when I'm in love. I'm there. I'm a hundred and ten percent. But I made an error. I cut myself off. From my strength. My strength did not come from loving on that pussy. I thought it did. But it didn't. My strength. Came from the sea. And those fucking dykes in Park Slope. They see it. They look at me. And they know. I don't belong. I'm not them. I've lost myself. But I can't get mad. I used to get mad, because I'd think—you know fuck you if you don't like me fuck you if I don't—like your fucking soy milk. Your fucking tea. But now I've realized. I can't be mad at them. They recognized I lost my strength. I cut myself off from the sea. I knew it when I saw "The Warriors" again last night. So I left.

CONSTRUCTION OF THE HUMAN HEART
Ross Mueller

Dramatic
Her, thirties to forties

Construction of the Human Heart is a play about writing a play. The characters, a married couple, are writers. Here, the woman speaks to her writing partner/husband. Tom is their son who died.

HER: I wanted to write something funny about you today. A bold imaginative story about the time I missed you the most . . . you went away to "Ballarat." Jesus. How exotic. Central character—young . . . middle aged . . . man—struggling to stay afloat. Searching for the secret to happiness. He resolves to travel the world on this quest, and basically—gets as far as Ballarat—on the train from Melbourne. He lives in a boarding house next to the railway line. His quest is beginning here at the Eastern Station Hotel. He examines people, makes notes, on what he thinks are the things that make the other residents happy. Keeps a journal on how they become—satisfied. I wanted to write this story from your perspective, from my perspective, from Tom's perspective . . . But—I stared at my screen in our freezing kitchen, and saw a bottle of whiskey and a bottle of vodka and so—and so I have come back to bed. Make up some poems instead. Something to make Tom laugh. "I like cuddles and I like hugs . . . But I hate—disgusting kisses. I love snuggles in bed with mum But I hate—disgusting kisses." Should be at school. He's not sick, he should be in a school yard somewhere. But he's not. I'm in bed. And you're drinking at Horacio's again—because you think I wanted you to leave me alone. I didn't. I just—I just gave you the impression that I didn't want you here. And you interpreted it to suit your own motivations. To escape. To run away . . . from me again. I have stopped for more than three and a half minutes and so—an image of you appears before me. You look . . . tired… but your image helps me. You are my scream saver…

(pause)

I can

(pause)

Please—he is here in the bed again. Help me.

Lawrence Harbison

Dramatic
Allison, forties

Allison tells her son about her clairvoyant aunt.

ALLISON: Aunt Aoife was born under the veil. That's what all my aunts used to cluck. Do you know what that means? She was born with the placenta wrapped around her head. Sometimes they are called a caulbearer. Caulbearers are very rare and it's rumored they have special powers. She had premonitions but never about anything too dramatic. Never life or death. Was it going to be a cold winter. Should you take the interstate or the parkway. She always knew when the locusts were coming. And she could touch things . . . Say your pocket watch wasn't working. She'd close her eyes and give it a little touch. A few days later you'd pull it out of your pocket and the hands are moving again. One time when you were a baby you were teething something awful. You had been crying for days, so much that your little baby vocal cords had grown hoarse and your cries took on a satanic quality. The doctors said it was just teething, natural. My moon was in Aquarius and anytime that happened I was supposed to go and see Aoife. So I bundled you up, my little screeching demon-spawn, and headed to the shore. When we arrived, she took one look at the bags under both of our eyes, smiled and touched you gently on the forehead with her open palm. You immediately stopped crying, closed your eyes and went to sleep. The two of us curled up on her sofa under an ancient patchwork quilt and had the deepest most complete sleep I have ever experienced.

Information on this playwright may be found at:
www.smithandkraus.com.
Click on the AUTHORS tab.

Seriocomic
Jenny, late thirties

Jenny has come to Cincinnati from New York to find her errant husband, Jack, who has mysteriously shown up at the house he grew up in, where his sister Lorna and his mother live after having, as it turns out, embezzled twenty-seven million dollars from the bank where he works. She is talking on the phone to a friend in New York, describing the décor of the kitchen.

JENNY: That's what he said! Can you believe that? "The truth is complicated." I'm thinking, not so complicated that they can't send you to jail, you jerk. Yes, I rea—I know, Stuart, but after everything I did for him, my family? My father! My father got him that job. Oh do not tell him I'm here, he will have an aneurysm if he—yes, I know, but of course I feel, I'm not—no, Jack's not here. I mean, he is here, I saw him, but he's not here right now. I walked in the front door, and before I could say three words there was this very convenient story about his father, and a kidney stone, and they all rushed off to some hospital. I mean, he did seem to be in some pain so what do I know, but I thought it was pretty coincidental, and I would not put it past Jack to actually give his father a kidney stone just to avoid dealing with this. He walked off with twenty seven million dollars from a major international financial institution, and nobody apparently can figure out how he did it. I think a kidney stone is relatively simple next to that. I know—I KNOW I sound ridiculous but I'm truly at my wit's end, Stuart. I've been sitting here for eight hours, by myself, in this house, why do people live in houses like this in the midwest, you should see this place. There actually is, seriously, linoleum floors. Linoleum, it's not a myth. And the cabinets are horrible. But get this: There are little ceramic plates on the walls with pictures painted on them, I'm not making this up. And the flatware is just, I don't understand it. I don't know what it's made of. Some sort of strange gray metal. Oh, oh, and the dishes are corelle. It says on the back of them: corelle. I don't know what "corelle" is, that's my point! It's just so deliberately without taste. And yes there are yards with grass and trees, Jack used to go on endlessly about all the grass and trees and air in the midwest but honestly I always found him to be needlessly smug about that stuff. Nature, like they invented nature. When they didn't invent it at all; let's face it, it's just here. Big deal. A fucking tree.

Information on this playwright may be found at:
www.smithandkraus.com.
Click on the AUTHORS tab.

Seriocomic
Mary, thirties to forties

*Mary's husband has been laid off. He claims to be starting
his own business, working from home. Here, she confides
to a neighbor how frustrating her life is.*

MARY: Its just I don't know how to help him. I'm at the
frayed edge of my wits. He gets to be home all day and
I don't get home until 6:45 because of the *fucking* traffic
on 694 and he's been home all day and I get home and
he's already on his first drink. He says it's his first drink
anyway. And he's cooked dinner which is of course very
sweet but then I say something about how his green beans
taste different my green beans you know like "oh these
taste different" just like that, not saying anything bad but
he drops his fork and I know he's offended and then it
starts. And I hate "NASCAR Unmasked and Personal"
and he knows I hate it I mean he's not a NASCAR kind
of guy he doesn't like NASCAR he just likes that show,
and he turns it on anyway while I'm finishing my dinner,
while I'm washing the dishes and he watches the TV
so fucking loud even the commercials and he laughs at
commercials, at *dumbfuck* commercials like the one with
the cartoon chicken getting rubbed down with chicken
magic.
  *(Mary imitates the commercial. It is a Latino
  Chicken.)*
"Ieeee! It tickles!" I mean Sharon its so *fucking crackass*
dumb. He says it helps him decompress, he's at the com-
puter all day long. And I'm like "doing what? Looking
at one of those titty websites? Live chatting with some
stripper lying on her crappy couch somewhere? How

long can a making a WEBSITE possibly take?" No. No I don't say that. I just think it. What I say is: "So how was your day? Did you bring the files to Kinkos" And he's like "No I forgot oh well I'll do it tomorrow" and I say "You know you can do it on their website through the file uploader, its super easy" And he says "Yes YES I know" and I say "well you know that book you bought for $65.00 said you've got to be hard on yourself about keeping to a schedule. Because Joe Blow down the street is also probably laid off, and also probably about to set up his dream business where you get to sit home all day and tell other people how to clean up the fucking financial wasteland of their day to day existence. And if Joe Blow gets his portfolio together before you do then Joe Blow gets the clients, not you." And he's says "Joe Blow can suck my nutsack"

    (pause for a moment, that word is like a bad taste in her mouth.)

And I say "oh that's a winning attitude." And then that's it—we're fighting and he's all "I'm trying to be proactive" and I'm all "today sucked, I barely got to eat lunch" and he's all "I'm afraid" and I'm like "don't say it like that" and he's like "look I have to put my beer on the floor! The photo album too!" And I'm like "that coffee table didn't go in this room . . . I want to live in a tent in the woods. With one pot and one pan. And an old fashioned aluminum mess kit with its own mesh bag. I want my hair to smell like the smoke from yesterday's fire, when I cooked my fish and my little white potatoes. I want to dry out my underwear on a warm rock. And feel the cold water rushing around my ankles, my feet pressing into the tiny stone bed that holds up the stream. Silver guppies nosing their heads into my calves . . .

Comic
Sharon, thirties to forties

Sharon is ranting to her neighbors about another neighbor who's been driving her nuts.

SHARON: Kenny you are not going to believe this I am fucking losing it do you see me I am losing it! It was the pink jogging suit lady. At our door! Only she wasn't wearing a pink jogging suit she was wearing shorts and a blue T shirt. And she came over to ask us politely—sort of—politely if we could keep our dog from shitting on her lawn. WE DON'T HAVE A DOG. And so I said to her, politely, I said "we don't have a dog" and she said "yes you do have a dog and it is quite fond of taking craps on my lawn." "Quite fond." Like slicing a razor blade across my face "quite fond". And I said "Lady, do you want to come in my house? We've got NOTHING in our house, especially a DOG. Especially we do not have a DOG." And she said "Listen, Missy." FUCKING MISSY! "Listen, Missy. I've lived in this neighborhood for 6 years, and I jog every morning. This dog appeared out of nowhere and started crapping on my lawn. I'm not asking you to get rid of it I'm just asking you to clean up his crap." And I practically started crying—look at me I'm crying now—and I said "Ma'am, people have accused me of many things before but they have never accused me of having a dog, you need to investigate further you need to knock on other doors—" And she said—her voice changed and she said "Look if it craps on my lawn one more time I am calling the police" and I said "Are you kidding? The police are going to fucking LAUGH IN YOUR FACE if you call them about some dogshit." And she said "AHA! So you DO have a DOG!"

And I said "No, no, no, no, no fucking NO there is no dog here lady!" And she just shook her head and kind of kicked our plant and said "Ha I thought it was fake." And turned around I mean FUCK. KENNY. FUCK. This is like FUCKED UP.

Comic

Natalia, thirties, Romanian (heavy accent)

Natalia is married to a Nigerian cab driver whom she passed on the street for seven days and fell in love with. They live in Pittsburgh with their infant son. Natalia has the gift of magic. She has a cure for everything except the mysterious illness that is killing her child, a boy who glows like the moon. Natalia keeps vigil by her son's bassinet and passes the time recounting all the stories and folk remedies she knows. In this moment, Natalia is waiting for her husband to return from work, however, he's been in a serious car accident that will leave him paralyzed. Although she has sensed that something bad has happened, she has pushed the thought away so as to keep things happy for the sake of the child.

NATALIA: When my husband is coming, huh? His turn to watch the baby. The boy likes his crazy stories. Is okay. I wait. I have no troubles with sleep. Sleep, don't sleep, I'm good. Peoples, Americans, they cannot go to sleep. Maybe's too much television, too much all-you-can eat buffet? Who can say?
   (To audience)
   Anybody asleep here? No? Not yet. Good. No snoring please. Bothers everybody. Especially the peoples with insomnia. I see this commercial, maybe you have too. A woman, she is not sleeping, and then next day doesn't like to hang balloon for birthday party? Guy says, Are you depressed? Trouble sleeping? Struggles with Anxiety? I'm thinking, maybe this woman come from my country. You know Romanian people saddest people in the world. Is true. They did study. Anyway in this commercial blue

pill is floating in the television with the butterfly wings. Happy floating pill, la la la, giving you night sweats, joint pains, suicidal thoughts and behaviors, leaking from the anus, liver damage, addictive over time, La la la, floating in the sky. Why peoples take this pill? You need sleep? Easy. Thirty minutes before the bedtime, eat one cookie. Just one.

(to audience member)

You. I mean it, just one. And one glass of milk. Trust me. I do this my whole life, I always sleep. Except for one time. Up all night. Lights on, lights off, twisting the sheets in bunches, making it straight, twisting it again. Everything. Six nights, crazy like this. This the week I fall in love with my husband. He meet me, he says he never sleeping better.

(Beat)

Now, where the fuck he is, I want my cookie.

Information on this playwright may be found at:
www.smithandkraus.com.
Click on the AUTHORS tab.

Dramatic
Sabine, mid-thirties

Time: Summer 2008

Setting: A hotel room in Trieste, Italy

Sabine, a Bosnian tourist in her mid-thirties has just spent the night with Andrej, a fisherman formerly of Bosnia. Sabine questions Andrej's role during their country's conflict.

SABINE: What did you do during the war? It was awful wasn't it? Sometimes I don't feel like being a nurse anymore, because I remember what I had seen, even today, even if my patient today will have a happy ending. It's hard to be so happy, but we have to, right, despite what we saw. And what did you see? I saw women, girls, some I knew, jump from the apartment buildings, those buildings you may have helped build, before the war, those buildings whose insides were blown apart, but whose roofs were amazingly intact, as if left, as a gift, to us, to find a way . . . to finish . . . what you had started, to end us. I saw the eyes of the women I performed abortions on, in the shelters of those bombed out roofless buildings, those raped and held and forced to be pregnant. I would walk, no, run. Run for my life, across the boulevards, through the roofless buildings, down the stairs, the broken stairs, into the shelters. I would say that too. "I don't see this. I don't hear it. I don't feel it. I'll do what I have to do to help those who need me, but I'm not one of them. I won't allow myself to be a part of this. A part of them." Is that how you survived? By forgetting you were . . . a part of them, but not a part of us. Us, being . . . the other? What did you see?

But everyone was doing it, right? Wearing a uniform. Wearing a ski mask over your face to hide, or perhaps to mask what you were truly feeling. You had to join the army, right? Become a nationalist? Hate us? Rape us? Kill us? What are you afraid of? Killing me now that you're finished and tossing me into the Adriatic Sea?

Information on this playwright may be found at:
www.smithandkraus.com.
Click on the AUTHORS tab.

Dramatic
Eden, twenties

Eden has come to Israel to find herself. Here, she is describing a dream, in which she realizes what she needs to do to find the meaning of her life.

EDEN: OH MY GOD! There was thunder and lightning; a dark gray sky, and a thick fog-like cloud covering the mountaintop. I heard the sound of a ram's horn shriek, and then everyone in the desert around me goes silent. It was electric. I am standing alone—amongst more 600,000 awakened souls; men, women and children standing side by side. I am close to the base of the mountain. I sense the energy of the people rising around me. I see light. Then, out of the light I see a figure. I know it is Moses. *(He's holding the Ten Commandments.)* And, then he sees me in the crowd. Moses looks right at me. Suddenly, like a super-hero with rubber arms, his arms stretch out above the crowd in front of me; and then Moses hands me the Ten Commandments. *(Pause)* They are really heavy. I feel the stone in my arms and I feel . . . like . . . they're mine. And, I feel . . . chosen . . . and then . . . I feel . . . terror. I wake-up. I see before me a lit forked-road. I know this is a once in a lifetime opportunity, a moment of communication from the other side. What if not taking this new road means searching in the wrong places and forever living with that gnawing feeling that comes from ignoring your dreams? What to do? Venture down a new, unknown road? Or ignore these sensations, and go back to sleep? The next day, I got on a bus to Jerusalem.

Information on this playwright may be found at:
www.smithandkraus.com.
Click on the AUTHORS tab.

Dramatic

Gloria, late forties-early to fifties

While driving her daughter Eden to the airport, Gloria lays into her for turning her back on marriage and a job making good money in the U.S. to go and live on a kibbutz in Israel.

GLORIA: That driver doesn't know where he's going. For that matter, neither do you. Stop your searching. It'll get you nowhere. Can't you see you're only two feet away from a pot of gold: marriage and a good job, and you're turning around and heading in exactly the opposite direction. You have one of the best business degrees in the world and, a hard working boyfriend who's going places. Do you think Adam is going to wait for you? We didn't raise you to be irresponsible. Do you ever think about anyone else, especially me? I'm here working day and night to pay for your education, and you're going on vacation. Working on a kibbutz, that's not working. Getting a job at a company in your own country, that's working. Your father and I have no intention of supporting you, so keep that in mind while you're picking peanuts on a kibbutz. In six months, you better be back on that plane to come home, or you'll be sorry. You don't come from the kind of family where you can just do what you want. Work is an important value to this family, because money is important. And with your degree you could be making real money, not peanuts on a kibbutz. Don't you even think about staying in Israel. When my parents told me to get married, I got married. When my parents told me to go to work, I went to work. I didn't just hop on a plane and take off and leave them. You can't do whatever you want. Get that idea out of your head. The family didn't expect you to work your whole life in the family business, like I did, but they did expect you to work somewhere. Your grandparents, aunts, uncles, even your great-aunts and great-uncles, they're all furious with *me* that you're not getting your career on track. They want to know who the hell you think you are? A princess? And remember, I am the one who gets judged by your actions. You better be careful, that's all I can say. Because I don't know what I'd do if there's a war over there or if something happened to you. Your father would be a wreck, and your grandparents, as well, for that matter. And I'd have to deal with them all. So you better consider that while you're over there, and the price that I'll have to pay if anything happens to you!

Information on this playwright may be found at:
www.smithandkraus.com.
Click on the AUTHORS tab.

Lawrence Harbison

FIX ME, JESUS
Helen Sneed

Seriocomic
Annabell, late twenties

Annabell is campaigning on behalf of a Democratic gu-
bernatorial candidate in Texas who has little chance of
winning because his opponent's name is David Crockett.
She is speaking from the pulpit of an African American
church, asking them to vote for her candidate, who defeated
an African American in the primary.

ANNABELL: I . . . I am . . . I stand . . . You may have noticed
there's a white person standing up here in your pulpit in
your church. It's amazing how white people just love
to go to black church at election time. Well, Reverend
Jefferson took pity on me and let me come before you
today. We're in trouble. There's an election on and I can't
get a single Democrat in Dallas to care. If things don't
change, I'm going to die of loneliness on November 5, or
get trampled to death by all those white people rushing
to vote for Davy Crockett. I work for your candidate, a
fine man named Walter Mapp. And yes, that's why I'm
here: To convince you to vote for him and the Democratic ticket. *(Pauses)* Look. This is the umpteenth time
a white person has come across town to ask for your
vote. My father's come to you before and now it's my
turn. But this year, something's different. I'm embarrassed because I'm here to ask you to compromise. You
had a supremely qualified candidate and I wish we were
one week out from electing Brenda Hawk the first black
governor of Texas. But we're not. We didn't get our first
choice. Everyone's saying both candidates are mediocre,
the evil of two lessers. *(Pauses)* How to explain this? My
grandmother passed away last Sunday. She was 84 and

had a long, vigorous life. She was quite a character—slept with a pearl-handled .22 pistol under her pillow because the Communists were coming. She was fierce. Hated the Russians, the Jews, the Chinese, the Catholics, gays, white trash, and uppity women. And boy, did she hate all of you. Didn't like me much, either. But. Last week, as she lay dying, she made one last demand. She insisted on voting absentee. We held her up to sign the ballot. Yes, my grandmother voted for every right wing nut on the ticket, and yes, she fought all the wrong battles, but she kept fighting until the minute she died. There's courage in that and I'm asking you to do the same. We can't stop fighting just because we didn't get our way. And we must take moral action, even when our hearts aren't in it. If we stay home, we lose. Besides, someone in this church needs to cancel out my grandmother's vote. On Election Day, your grandmother is exactly as powerful as mine. November 5 may be the only day of pure justice coming your way. Don't you dare miss it. Vote for Walter Mapp. Vote Democratic. Vote for your grandmother, your children, yourself. Close your eyes and pretend it's for Barbara Jordan if you have to! Look, Ronald Reagan has turned America from a nation that *does* good into a nation that *feels* good. We Democrats must do better. The Republicans have plucked this thin-lipped white boy out of West Texas, where there aren't any black people—and just because his name is Davy Crockett, every white person in Texas is going to vote for him. Well, the original Davy Crockett was just some redneck cracker from Tennessee who was dumb enough to get killed at the Alamo. Why on earth would we want to elect another one? People of color brought down the first Davy Crockett. You can defeat this one, too. "Remember the Alamo" will have a whole new meaning. Thank you. God bless you. Remember the Alamo!

Information on this playwright may be found at:
www.smithandkraus.com.
Click on the AUTHORS tab.

Comic
Alex, twenty-three

Alex is a "Barista Extraordinaire." This is her own personal Seven Ages of Man speech.

ALEX: *(to Audience)* A trap: The Seven Ages of Remote Control Man. At first the infant, it doesn't matter what they put in front of you, purple dinosaurs, talking animals, puffy clouds, as long as it moves, blinks and makes noise, it's good television. And you have NO control over the remote. Then the school kid, it's the battle between your little super-ego and your little id: PBS numbers and letters vs. Cartoon Network hammer hits and booger jokes. And your parents tend to have the remote. Then as you slide into puberty, you grab the control and it's reality shows, music videos, clothes, sex, music, sex, skin-care, sex, slang, sex, sex, sex, sex, sex, and then POP, you're out into the working world it's News and Wall Street Channels at the office by day and by night it's sitcoms and crime dramas where you learn life lessons in 22 or 44 minutes. Unless it's "American Idol" where you learn your life lesson by having a bunch of fans who can text. And then some Comedy Central, late night T.V. to bed. But you put on a few years, you find yourself drawn into your niche, your rut, your "lifestyle", your ESPN, your HGTV, C-SPAN, History Channel, Cooking Channel, until suddenly you're old. And you find yourself watching the Weather Channel—actually watching the Weather Channel as your default, or just having it on in the background because it's . . . comforting . . . to know there's weather happening . . . somewhere . . . And then last stage of all, that ends this viewing history, is second childhood where you'll stare at pretty much anything as long as it moves, blinks, and makes noise. And once again someone else has control of the remote. Don't let this happen to you.

Comic
Alex, twenty-three

Alex tells us about the typical male denizens of coffee shops.

ALEX: *(to Audience)* Okay, right? Yes. He's cute. I know. Great. But that's about as big a trap as staring at the T.V. all night. They both encourage you to put down roots and stay and just . . . stare. But especially boys, cute boys, intriguing cute boys, intriguing cute boys who are artists and can think on their feet . . . they can be even more dangerous because if you get attached to them you can screw the whole delicate ecosystem we've set up here.

> *(Begins working as she talks.)*

See, the basic building blocks of life in a coffee house are the "In-and-Outs", the ones who know what they want, get it and go, constantly churning the air, the coffee, the baked goods. "In-and-Outs" come in a variety of specimens: The Hard Hats, The Chilled Cops, The Starving Students. It's easy to take these organisms for granted, but without that constant turning over everything else dies. And without them you wouldn't get to the truly interesting species: For instance, the Recoverus Addicti—A.A., heroin, cigs, you name it. You have the best chance of seeing them at dawn, they've already been up for hours and are just happy to have somewhere to go and someone to talk to. A lot. And an off-shoot of this species is the Odiferous Coagulatoria, the five old guys camping out in the corner ordering nothing or next to nothing, because they can subsist on talk about communism, poetry, and how they'd fix the universe, which they'd stand a better chance of doing if they'd take the occasional shower. Your dilemma with them is, are you sympathetic and let them grow or business like and weed'em out? 'Cause they spread like kudzu. Communist philosopher kudzu. And they come into conflict with the Laptopus Americanus, recognizable by their business wear, they come in and build nests, setting out whole work-stations and commencing to create new worlds while ingesting upscale drinks and muffins. They share the same markings as the Americanus Lonely, but the latter aren't on company time—they just write letters, do the crossword, read the newspaper—all things they could do at home, but at home they'd be alone. So they're here. And beside them are the Maternia Escapus, middle-aged females, the occasional male, who have dropped their offspring off . . . somewhere . . . and are now sharing news and mating rituals over lattes and teas. And flying above all this are the Biker Boyum, the couriers who dart in, grab a drink, scan the newspaper and are out the door for a day of running words and objects to the larger world, carrying your cup, your brand, your seed out with them like bees with pollen drifting from their legs. And then you have the midges and gnats of the world: the Frat Boys and Sorority Sisters who tend to be visible only at night and on weekends, ordering French Vanilla Cappuccinos—which don't exist, French Vanilla is an ice cream, not a coffee—so you make them something lethal like a Chocolate Mocha or Caramel Cooler Machiatto, and they survive it because they haven't eaten in a week. But they all—the whole system—flows together, feeds on each other, builds and collapses a thousand times a day. And you can't start injecting new species or new relationships, now matter how cute the boy, because it really is . . . a perfectly balanced system . . .

Dramatic
Sylvia, early to mid-thirties, African-American

Sylvia is talking to her father, a retired star NFL lineman. Sylvia's estranged husband Ronnie, a former star NFL running back, disappeared and, after many months of addled, wandering homelessness, has recently been found dead, a suicide from drinking antifreeze. She has been asked by a man who works for an organization which studies deceased football players in order to determine the effects of football contact on their brains to sign papers consenting to allowing them to examine Ronnie's brain for signs of Chronic Traumatic Encephalopathy. Her father is adamantly opposed to cooperating with the man. Sylvia was too—until she begins to wonder if her own father might be suffering from CTE.

SYLVIA: You've given me three pairs of the same heels over the last three months. Now maybe that's just 'cause you love these shoes so much, but judging by your face I don't think that's the reason.
    (Beat)
I didn't want to say anything. I almost didn't, but . . . I tried to think that it was just an accident, just a coincidence, but then I realized . . . it's that you don't remember giving them to me. And that's when I signed and faxed the papers. You don't remember giving them to me. Three times? You put milk in the cabinet sometimes. Fresh milk. I put it back in the fridge. You leave the cap off. I put it back on. I clean up after you. I do the grocery shopping so you don't buy six bags of marshmallows. I hope you're just absentminded. I hope you're just getting old. I hope Ronnie just suffered depression for some unexplained,

unconnected reason. That hitting his head against the ground and against other helmets ten or twenty thousand times had nothing to do with his downward spiral. But I know it did.

(Beat)

Yes, football paid for this house and my ring and all three pairs of these shoes. But now we have to pay for football. And you might say that the only thing you care about is winning, but what's the point of winning if you can't remember that you won?

Information on this playwright may be found at:
www.smithandkraus.com.
Click on the AUTHORS tab.

Dramatic
Janet, forties

Janet is married to Harry an English Professor at a nearby university. Harry has recently been stricken by an odd malady where he has bouts of "fury"; his arms start swinging violently in an unpredictable and uncontrollable striking motion. In one recent occurrence, Harry accidently hit his wife, Janet. In the monologue, Janet is speaking to her brother Derek, who is a psychiatrist for the "guilty rich", i.e. people who are in search of being exonerated. Derek proffers that Harry's illness is a symptom of growing American anger, and has just asked Janet if she plans on leaving Harry. They are at the boxing gym where Harry takes refuge.

JANET: I'm not leaving him. Or I don't think I'm leaving him. It's more like he's leaving me. Since he hit me, he won't sleep in our room. He sleeps in the guest room. He handcuffs one arm to the bed and throws the key out into the hallway so that only I can set him free. And this place, he almost lives here now. He pays them three times their membership fee, because he comes in at short notice and he takes the ring. They actually kick clients out to make room for him when he needs it. They think it's cool. 'If Rocky and the energizer bunny had a kid . . . ' —that sort of thing. And Harry thinks it's the only place he's not a freak. He was here seven hours yesterday, and he cancelled a graduate thesis review today. He says he can tell when it's going to be a rough day. Not when the fury actually comes . . . the fury . . . that's what he calls them. Sort-of the anti-rapture. He hides. He waits for the next fury to happen, he stays till he's so exhausted and so mentally defeated that he feels it won't happen for a while. Then he comes home, we eat dinner, we try to talk about it—but what are we even talking about?—we don't know why it's happening. And then when he finally starts to feel rested, it worries him—so he kisses me goodnight, goes to the guest room and handcuffs himself to the bed.

Seriocomic
Roberta, twenties to thirties, African American

ROBERTA: Hello hello hello my brothers and sisters, y'all
got a second for W.I.L.D, the ice-cold-red-hot-new-shit
you gotta get with, just one second in one second Roberta's gonna turn your whole world around, hot day
outside today, HOT day, step right up and cool off in the
knowledge of the ever-expanding-mind-blowing-heart-
stopping wow, now, YES it is hot as hell outside, YES
we got a lunatic in the White House using your money
to wipe his ass, YES our mothers are mourning our
brothers down in Vietnam dropping bomb after bomb
after bomb, YES Judy Garland is DEAD, but we are
ALIVE my brothers and sisters, let us not mourn, let us
be reborn, can I get a witness *(Amen)* sock it to me now
all right. I'm here all week, people! I'm big, I'm black,
and you can bet your ass I'm hard to ignore, W.I.L.D on
the loose, truth on the loose, hold me back now!

Information on this playwright may be found at:
www.smithandkraus.com.
Click on the AUTHORS tab.

HIT THE WALL
Ike Holter

Seriocomic
Roberta, twenty to thirties

ROBERTA: Yeah, that's right, get-to-stepping cause I'm out
here starting a revolution while y'all just shit-shooting
bad-groovin' and prostituting, uh-huh that's right,
WALK!
(They're gone.)
So! Hey! This is Wild, and Wild stands for Women Internationally Learning Divisiveness. You dig, all-right,
check it: We're all about women internationally learning divisiveness. Right? Right on, sister. Now this isn't
one of those "sit around in a circle holding hands crying
about our Mommies" things you see over at NYU, nuh-
uh, we're not about the love in, we're about the love-ing
with-in, (you feel me?) we're about looking inside of
ourselves, getting to know that, respecting that, love-ing
with-in that, and then looking outside of ourselves and
going "Say WHAT now? HELL no. Things gotta change,
I mean DAMN!" You feel me? You feel me. Baby, this
is about Women Internationally Learning Divisiveness
. . . . (And if you take that to mean two sisters getting
to know each other in the process, go ahead and go with
it.) OK! Now I'm gonna talk about the man. First rule of
WILD: "Fight the man." And not the man as in the man
with the plan, the man ever-present and always above,
the man who is with-in, love-ing, Jesus Christ, hell no,
not that man, the man I'm talking about is the man with
the book, not the good book, the book that gets thrown,
I'm talking about the man with the bat, the pigs, cause
you know what the Second rule of WILD is? We ain't
afraid of no cops, we don't believe their lies, we slash
their tires when they start acting up, making em slow
down, making em think twice, now can you shovel what

Lawrence Harbison   75

I'm digging sister? This is about looking BEYOND our-selves, with-in, love-ing, see now I knew you felt me, OK, the final rule of WILD? You ready for this? Final Rule of Wild—Do not trust the gays. They rile shit up. They're loud, they're crazy, and I know you know the reason we got so many police shuffling around parks is cause they can't keep their peens in their pants. (Also they don't share their green which makes me PISSED; damn selfish-ass fairy-fuckers,) So I'm here here to tell you that if Women are to learn how to achieve Divisive-ness Internationally, we gotta say "hold it boys, we're driving this next revolution, you can sit shotgun if you're so excited, but don't you dare tell us directions because we know exactly where we going so put the map down and maybe turn the music up so we can get our groove on, OK?" Damn the man. Fuck the pigs. Hold off the boys. Those are the rules. What'd you think?

Information on this playwright may be found at:
www.smithandkraus.com.
Click on the AUTHORS tab.

Dramatic
Roberta, twenties to thirties, African American

ROBERTA: Ok look, I don't call myself a lesbian, I call myself a dyke don't call me a lesbian, my Grandma was a lesbian. No, but you know what I mean! That word's over, done, dead, bury it in the back. We gotta start standing up for ourselves, taking the words they throw at us, and owning them. I'm a dyke. I'm a nigger. I'm a woman, what else you got, bring it on, say it to me . . . Ok—Ok, *I'm not allowed* to go to Women's Movement meetings anymore? Alright but it's not my fault, it's not my fault alright cause *all I cause I told them* was that their march speeches should include some diversification within their administration, They said "No, no, no, Roberta, the movement is too fragile," Expected me to take that; I said "You tell me when the movement is stronger, cause I'm gonna join an organization that's about EQUAL rights, COMPASSIONATE politics, UNIVERSALITY." . . . . So I went to the Black Panthers. And the Black Panthers hated me more than the Women's Movement! They can't screw me, so they don't wanna see me, hahaha, they . . . Look I know this is crazy, you're sitting here, with a one-woman-coalition, somebody who nobody wants, I know, it's bonkers, but . . . . but this is all I have. This is about being the best, proudest, strongest women you can be, the woman you know you can be, the woman you deserve to be.

Information on this playwright may be found at:
www.smithandkraus.com.
Click on the AUTHORS tab.

HONKY
Greg Kalleres

Comic
Andie, twenties, white

Andie is in her bedroom talking to her fiancée, Peter.

ANDIE: Oh, my parents called! They want to know what
we're doing for the holidays. I said I'd ask you, but I
think they want us to go up to Connecticut. They're
gonna have the Brennans up. Remember the Brennans?
Mr. Brennan's the one who always smells like Mayon-
naise. Apparently, they're family now! For the past few
months my parents have begun referring to them as
Aunt and Uncle for some reason. Oh, that reminds me,
I haven't told you this yet because my therapist and I are
still kind of working it out but I'm pretty sure I have a
repressed memory of Mr. Brennan touching me as a kid.
I mean, it's repressed, so you never know for sure, but I
get a queasy, after school special type of feeling around
him. And whenever he sees me in a bathing suit he gives
me this very specific sort of: "Whoa, I think I may have
molested you once" kind of look. Plus when I go to sleep
in my old house, I have this immediate craving for a
turkey sandwich. You know. Turkey? Mayo? Probably
means nothing but my therapist is gonna think about it.
So, anyway, Mom asked the other day if we wanted Mr.
Brennan to do our wedding service because he's some
sort of judge and I was like, "are you kidding?" Can you
see us up there saying our vows and I suddenly smell
Miracle Whip and have a panic attack?!

Serio-comic
Emilia, thirties, Black

Emilia is a black therapist. Her white patient, Peter, is consumed with guilt over a sneaker commercial he wrote that may have inspired the shooting of black kid. Until now, Emilia she has struggled to repress all her racist thoughts toward him. But when Peter explodes, telling her he's sick of feeling guilt for being white, Emilia can't take it anymore.

EMILIA: And Charley Cross? Are you sorry for him too? That's funny. I thought that was the entire reason you were in therapy. A 14 year old African American boy shot in the face because of a commercial.

(beat)

Imagine me listening to a man apologize over and over without the first clue as to what he's sorry for. He thinks it's because he's white. Well. Isn't that a shame. Even his contrition is out of context. His shame, ignorant and irresponsible.

(beat)

This was never therapy. It was a confession. To the only black person you know. And you thought if we went out, if you charmed me and we connected as people it would somehow magically pardon you of all wrong doing. An instant hall pass that would walk you past every negro you meet with a fist bump.

(beat)

I come in here every day and listen to the problems of white folks. Crackers with cracker problems and cracker guilt! I tell myself to be objective. Listen to the issues. Be understanding. "They're not white people," I say, "they're people with problems." But after a while it doesn't take. No matter how many pills I swallow, it doesn't suppress. But this is my job. To tolerate it. To pretend, like you, that I understand. That I don't seethe with my own disgust. My own shame. But the problem, Peter, is that I do understand. Your fortunate problems? I get it. I too am unscathed. Untouched. Like you. So, I donate to the NAACP and I volunteer to the United Negro College Fund. And I do it all to absolve myself. Ignorantly. Out of context. Just. Like. You. So, you see, you came to the wrong nigger for exoneration. You feel ashamed for your whiteness? So do I, Peter. So do I.

Dramatic

Magda, mid-twenties

Magda's brother Chad has just finished telling her a fragmented story illustrating his growing sense of isolation from society, in the hopes of momentarily connection and receiving her sympathy. Magda responds by changing the subject and talking about herself.

MAGDA: Is this a signal? Am I supposed to do something? 'Cause I don't know what that would be, if it is.

(Pause.)

Hey, good news? I'm quitting. I'm telling Sheila tomorrow. Maybe even right now if I can get my ass over there. Not 'cause of you, I was gonna do it anyway. In case you're worried you fucked things up for me. Otherwise you would have. But lucky for you I'd already decided on a new path. Halfway to Charlie's I'm thinking about how, yeah, I'm broke, and how excited I got when you gave me that money, and how fucking *sad* that is? And I'm like "This is some desperate shit." And Charlie's revelation was totally a sign. I'm like "Yeah. That's *enough* of that." All the useless bullshit. All the names and the pathetic eyes. Hey, sweetheart. Babe. Hottie, cutie, babyfuckin-doll. I'll have another, another, another . . . Echo! Day in, day out, like a clock. The clock follows you home, gets in under the sheets with you. In your dreams . . . Hey, hey: Are you too drunk to drive me over there tonight? You wouldn't even have to go inside, just wait for me with the engine running. You're letting me borrow it? What? You're *giving* me your car? I'll take them, so don't fuck with me. I'll have it back in one piece. I don't know how it is the days start for some people at eight, some at nine, some in the middle of the afternoon . . . We're all supposed to turn back into . . . dust. Hey, I think I'm gonna get Daddy some of those wireless TV headphones for Christmas this year. He's sick of me complaining about the noise, I'm sick of the noise, win-win.

   (Beat.)

You're a pretty good older brother, you know? You never gave me any shit I couldn't get over.

Dramatic
Magda, mid-twenties

Magda has just discovered that her brother, Chad, having left home two years previously, has snuck back home and is hiding in the under-sink kitchen cabinet. The most important thing to her at this moment is that Carmine, who moved in the night Chad left, and has since taken his place in the household, not discover that Chad has returned. At this very moment, Carmine is heading directly for the cabinet—Magda stops him dead by absurdly screaming "Mr. Kaishan!" and then ad-libbing a story to distract him:

MAGDA: Woodshop. The year I graduated? That was his retirement year. Last day of school? Bell rings, he won't let us go. He's all "No, wait, not yet." We're all, *C'mon!* Summer! Eternity! Right? But none of us move, because we all know this is, like, his *whole* life. And he goes: "Now, before you all run off to the rest of your lives, I wanna show you something *really* amazing, something you can *really* take with you." And he grabs a two by four, or whatever, and he goes over to the bandsaw, that's a thing, right? And he goes: Watch this. And he puts the board down onto the thing and he turns the saw on and he's talking but nobody can hear what he's saying—the bandsaw and . . . everyone's got earplugs—guy's a total health and safety freak, you know?—and he runs the two by four through the bandsaw, and there this explosion of blood, and he stops pushing the board through the saw, and he holds up his hand and he's missing a finger and his hand is shooting blood all over the place, and he just stares at it, and then he turns off the bandsaw, and it's all wahwahwahwahwahwah wah wah waaaaahhhh . . . and nobody knows what to do, we all just start taking out our earplugs, and he says: "That's not what I meant to do." And he stares at his hand, and it looks like he's trying to shoot himself in the face with a really fucked up water gun, and he screams at us: "Put your goddamn earplugs back in!" And we do. And he turns the bandsaw back on: wah wah wah wahwahwah wahwahwahwah . . .! and starts running the two by four through a *second* time and there's this *second* explosion, and he drops the two by four and stares at his hand, which now has two fingers missing, and more blood's shooting all over the place, and he doesn't shut the bandsaw off this time, he just starts talking to all of us again, pointing his fucked up water gun at the ceiling, and still NO ONE can hear what he's SAYING!

(Beat)

Dramatic
Ria, late thirties-early forties, Caribbean

Ria is haunted by her past. She looks back at a dark and turbulent moment in her life, and is determined to tell her husband everything, especially what his temporary loss of memory has erased.

RIA: It was because of your time in Milan that you surrendered to God. And I found you and not God. It's only recently that I started to remember. I remember the lies of a German man. He promised me love and to make me into a model in Italy. He told me that Italians were crazy about Caribbean girls that looked like me. He paid for my trip to Italy. In Milan is where my nightmare began. A couple named Günter and Winola picked me up at the airport. They told me that the German couldn't come for me because he had to travel to Munich. They told me I would stay with them until he got back. So when we got to their place, Günter pointed a gun at me and took me to a room. The German man turned out to be a human trafficker and he had sold me like a slave. Two days after that I was sold to another man, an Italian man, who had a brothel on the outskirts of the city. From then on I was forced to give myself to strangers against my will. Then one day you came to my rescue. You told me there was something about me that made me different. You said that I put you in turmoil. You told me there was something about me that changed you. And you saved me from that hell.

Information on this playwright may be found at:
www.smithandkraus.com.
Click on the AUTHORS tab.

I THINK I LOVE YOU
Sharon Goldner

Comic
Siboban, twelve

*Siboban is a precocious pre-teen who is a gifted artist—
but she's more interested in the latest teen heartthrob. This
used to be Jack Wild, but now he's David Cassidy of The
Partridge Family.*

SIBOBAN: I'm in love. You probably don't think anything
   of it because I'm just a kid and you wonder, just how
   real can it be, that I've got so much more living to do,
   but that just means you're old and you've forgotten. I
   will never forget what it's like to be a kid when I grow
   up. That's the problem with adults. The dementia doesn't
   start when you're ancient; it starts as soon as you're not
   a kid anymore.
   (Pause)
   At first I was in love with Jack Wild. He's that English
   actor who was Academy Award-nominated for *Oliver*. I
   didn't love him then; I didn't even know him then. But
   after that he was on *Pufnstuf*. He was this kid named
   Jimmy who had a golden flute and he lands in this place
   called Living Island where everything is alive the way
   humans are, like the trees even talk. It's all one great big
   trippy place, and the evil witch, Witchiepoo, wants that
   golden flute. In every episode, she concocts some crazy
   plan to get it and Jimmy and Pufnstuf, the dragon mayor
   of Living Island, foil her plans. My friend Michelle and I
   were in love with Jack Wild. You can call it a crush, and
   maybe it looks that way to adults, but it shouldn't be that
   easily dismissed. Our loves flatten us out just the same
   as yours do you. So one day I'm grooving on Jack Wild
   and Michelle comes over and says, "We love *him* now,"

and she smacks down a teen magazine folded to a picture of David Cassidy. It was before *The Partridge Family* even aired their first episode. So, I look at him and he's okay and all, but I say to Michelle, "What about Jack?" and she says, "We don't like him anymore." Now, before you consider me a follower, I've got to say that Michelle comes with some pretty good credentials: she may be a whole year younger than me but she's the youngest of four sisters, and she's got boobs already. I'm not talking your beginning double A's, mind you—I am talking down-the-alphabet cups, like a D. I'm not jealous. My day will come, I mean, everyone gets boobs, don't they? There are even a few male teachers at school with what look like boobs. So I'm just waiting for mine.

Information on this playwright may be found at:
www.smithandkraus.com.
Click on the AUTHORS tab.

I THINK I LOVE YOU
Sharon Goldner

Comic
Siboban, twelve

Siboban is a precocious pre-teen. She's crazy about David Cassidy of The Partridge family. Her friend Michelle has moved on from unattainable teen heartthrobs like David to a boy in their school.

SIBOBAN: Michelle likes Mickey Abramovitz now. What, you haven't heard of Mickey A.? That's what she calls him. You haven't heard of him because he's nobody you would have ever heard of. Mickey A's just a boy at school. Michelle has moved on from the glossy pages of *Tiger Beat* and *16 Magazine* to the high-end gloss of oily skin, pimples, poor attempts at shaving, and Adam apples that should really be called Adam's nuts because the voice they produce cracks so much.
     (Pause)
I meant nuts like peanuts. Not, you know, the other kind. That's what the boys call their, you know, down there place. So Michelle is with Mickey A. now. She gave me all of her David Cassidy posters and magazines. I didn't understand why she can't like them both, and she said, "This is not Utah, Siboban." I realize that, of course. Because of Donny Osmond. He's on the teen magazines, too. He's a Mormon, but he only has one mother. He's not my type. Too goody two-shoes. I tried to get Michelle back on board, but she wasn't interested. She and Mickey A. got all the way to second base recently. I wasn't sure what that was exactly, I mean, I always strike out when we play softball in gym. I've never made it even to first base. But then, Michelle cleared that up for me, and I realized, I've never made it to first base that way either.

They stuck their tongues in each other's mouths. Gross! I can't imagine doing that. I had to rethink all of those romantic kisses on my mother's soap operas once I knew what they were doing inside their mouths. Michelle says that's why you close your eyes when you're doing it, so you don't have to think about it.

Information on this playwright may be found at:
www.smithandkraus.com.
Click on the AUTHORS tab.

Lawrence Harbison

Comic
Nina, early thirties, African American

Nina is a friend of Jesse (who has not yet revealed to everyone that he's gay), who has told her she should come to Minneapolis, where he lives. She's not interested. He's asked her what's wrong with Minneapolis.

NINA: Ahmo pretend you ain't jis sed dat. Chicago got flavor. Chicago got color. It's all segregated, but it's here. When I first landed, I took the blue line to the red line to the bus and I saw so many fine ass women I thought I was bout ta fall out. I saw Black girls, Latinas, Asians, Arabians,—Dots *and* Feathers, Blatinas, Blasians, Blatasians, Blarabians, Blindians, Blatindians, Europeans, Bleuropeans, Bleurasians, Bleutarasians, Maroons, Octaroons, Quadroons—OH! I saw this thick bitch walking down the street after I got off the trainnnnnnn. Juicy. Just juice. All juice. Lips. Hips. I wanted to stick a straw in the bitch and sip her. So, I asked her where she thought she was goin' and she came at me with this sexy accent—I said, "Girl, where you from? Tunisia? Madagascar or some shit?" And she said—"America. I'm American . . ." and I said "Well, God Bless yo' American ass!"

Information on this playwright may be found at:
www.smithandkraus.com.
Click on the AUTHORS tab.

Dramatic
Mary (played by Mahari in the play)

Mary appears as if in a dream to her son Jesus, who has run off to India to try and escape his fate back in Galilee. She talks to him as if he were her betrothed, Joseph.

MARY: My parents say there's a way to get rid of it, they insist, they're scared, Joseph of course so am I but I don't want to do what they're asking. They say there's a man in Jerusalem who can give me a drink that will make it go away, so before they find him I need you to take me away. My dreams say you were chosen too, chosen by God to raise this boy as his own, to teach him what it is to be a man, so one day he can be much much more than that. Joseph, please. I don't want to drink the drink they want me to, if you take me away then I'll know it was an angel who spoke to me, that it was the Word of God. But if you can't, then I'll know it wasn't an angel but a devil, if I can't have you with me, then I will beat my loins with a rock until the curse falls out of me and back to the ground beneath. Marry me, Joseph. If you come with me, and take me to bed, despite not being the first to do so, then I'll know that the first was God. I worry it was the devil. If you marry me, Joseph, then I will live certain in the knowledge that we will be saved. By the child. Joseph, saved by the child.

*Information on this playwright may be found at:
www.smithandkraus.com.
Click on the AUTHORS tab.*

JESUS IN INDIA
Lloyd Suh

Dramatic
Abigail, late teens

Abigail and Jesus travelled to India together. She loves him, but he dumped her so she went back him to Galilee. Now she has returned, with a plea to him to return home with her.

ABIGAIL: You're probably wondering how I found you, but you wouldn't believe me if I told you, I almost don't believe it myself. I think I should just say what I have to say and see what happens. I will, I'll just say it. But first maybe I should . . . no, focus, Abigail, come on, focus you stupid bitch. DON'T SAY ANYTHING because before you do there's more I have to say and I had it all rehearsed in my mind because there's a sequence to it, and the sequence is important because things have happened, things are still happening, that are more, NO!, shut up you dumb whore just tell him! God just tell him you fat bitch, I mean what the hell! Your father died.
    Silence.
Your father's dead, Jesus. Joseph is dead. Murdered. It's all such a mess, back home, there's hardly home left. It's gone from chaos to cataclysm, the Romans have overrun everything, they destroy our buildings, invade our homes, desecrate our temples and steal our people into slavery. But there's a resistance. And I'm a part of it. We've fought, we fight, your mother and I, along with others, I would have come sooner but every pair of hands is needed, every voice and every committed will, there are so few working on behalf of the Jews. I came because we need you. Your father wasn't a fighter. He wasn't a zealot, didn't cause any trouble. He was just

there. You know? He was just a man. And they cut him down anyway, like they cut down many who are just men. Your people are dying, Jesus. We are fighting and we are losing and we are dying,
   Silence.
We need you. It's time. Jesus, it's time to come home.

JIHAD JONES AND THE KALASHNIKOV BABES
Jussef El Guindi

Comic
Cassandra, twenties to thirties

*Cassandra is an actress in a movie which is nothing but
a mass of anti-Muslim clichés. She doesn't care and she's
miffed that her co-star, Ashraf, is. He has principles—she
doesn't.*

CASSANDRA: So you're miffed you're not playing a boffo
    character with a great personality and charm to spare.
    Well, boo-hoo. My pussy weeps for you. Excuse me
    while I break out the tissues for another struggling actor
    asked to play shit and make it real. What the hell kind
    of business do you think this is? An academy for the
    study of human behavior? This is the land of gummy
    bears and popcorn; and making out in the back row and
    leaving a mess for the ushers to clean up. It ain't deep;
    it's not real, and if you're lucky you get paid a whole lot.
    Shove it. I don't want to hear it. Save it for after I leave.
    Do you think I got to where I am today because I was
    picky? I'm *a woman*. Do you know what I get offered
    as *a woman*? In a business that prizes eye-candy before
    everything else? Boobs and ass before character and
    content? Honey: the pickings are slim. I get my choice
    of whores, skanks, saints or virgins. And that's when I'm
    not being offered whores, skanks, saints or virgins. Or
    bitches. Or warrior princesses with penis envy. Or any
    combination of the above. The trough is full of swill, hon,
    and always has been, and if you're lucky you find one or
    two great nuggets in your career and that's what you live
    off while you forage through more trash. Stereotypes,
    please. You don't know anything about stereotypes till
    you've walked in my hooker boots for six weeks on a
    movie set. Get over it. I know my part isn't great. But I'm

going to give it everything I have and make those pimply kids in back row stop tonguing for two minutes and give me their full sex-crazed attention because goddamn it I deserve it. And if you've got any balls, you'll take this part and do the same. Jesus. You're an actor. Act like one you little piss-ant. You all think on that while I go make some calls. And when I get back, if you're not finished agonizing over whatever it is you've got your boxers in a twist about, then—I'm gone.

Information on this playwright may be found at:
www.smithandkraus.com.
Click on the AUTHORS tab.

Dramatic
Olga, thirties

Olga is speaking to Alexanochkin, a KGB interrogator who has been trying to get her to denounce her lover, Boris Pasternak, who based the character of Lara in Doctor Zhivago on her.

OLGA: Everything that the government did to punish him . . . All of it came from me. I led you to the publishers . . . and to the Writers Union . . . Cornered him into refusing the Prize . . . Your colleague Semionov made it clear that if I didn't comply, our fates would be even worse. I had to protect Pasternak. And the only way I could think of doing that was to betray him . . . to betray *Doctor Zhivago.* Now there's no one else left to defend them. A book is more than just ink and paper Comrade, and a novel is not merely a story, at least this one isn't. *Doctor Zhivago* is a testament to the individual fighting to exist in a society that only values the collective. It is an indictment, not just of a system that betrayed the people it was created to protect, but also of human loneliness and isolation. It is a paean to love . . . love that can survive the bloody collapse of one civilization and endure the messy birth of the next. You ask me if I am Lara. Lara did not betray Yuri . . . not in life and certainly not in death. So I guess you finally have the answer to your question.
(Pause)
Doctor Zhivago is his legacy. More than even his poetry. More than his life. More than his children or his wife or his mistress.
(By "mistress," she is referring to herself.)
This is his monument to Russia. To the country he loves.

So long as it exists, it can be read . . . and Yuri and Lara and his poetry . . . the Revolution . . . It will all matter again. Maybe it will only matter to that one person. But that was always the point, wasn't it?

Information on this playwright may be found at:
www.smithandkraus.com.
Click on the AUTHORS tab.

Seriocomic
Jane, late thirties-early forties

Jane Forge, a high-powered Hollywood talent agent, is on the phone with the producer of one of her star client's recent summer box office blockbusters. The producer is trying to get out of having to pay her client a contractual 20% back-end gross fee.

JANE: Seymour. Seymour, listen. Listen to me, Sey. Listen, Seymour, I don't care how far back we. This is your problem. No, no, no, no. Well, how would you like it if I shoved a ball gag in your mouth, and then fucked you up the ass with a giant strap-on, because that's what this is beginning to feel like. No, that is not. That's not. That is not what we agreed upon, Seymour, and what's more you know it. We agreed, listen, listen, we. We agreed, what we agreed upon was this, we agreed on two for the first, and four for the second, and if by some miracle there happened to be a third, what we agreed on was six. Now, you're telling me that because. Well, that's not my problem, Seymour, you signed a contract, and I hate to break it to you but the contract clearly states twenty percent. That's twenty percent of box office. Listen to me very carefully, Seymour. I could give a good assfuck about how far over budget you may think you are. Point is, you should've thought of that before you inked the goddamn deal. That's fine, Seymour, but know that if you do decide to take this thing to court then I'm gonna have your balls in a jar on a shelf in my trophy case before you can even get granted an automatic stay. Because I know the fucking judge, that's how. Comprende? Good. Goodbye.

Dramatic
Jane, late thirties to early forties

JANE: Hey, don't get up with me, kiddo. Not right now. You got it? I needed us to be a united front in here with him, but instead. Whatever. All it means is I now have to negotiate within even more constrained parameters than I did previous, understand? Good. Now, let's talk about this. I was never opposed to. I wasn't. This, I mean, think about it. The more your face is out there. The more people are reminded that you exist. It's good press. For you, for me, for the movie, for whatever else it is you plan on spending the rest of your life doing. This will ensure for you longevity. I was never opposed to the idea of you doing a talk show, Tom. What I was opposed to was the particular talk show you chose to use as a launching pad. One mistake, one slip-up, and you won't need a fucking egg timer to clock how long it'll take you to go from being money in the bank to being the next big Hollywood cocktail party joke. Which, let me assure you, is not something that producers and casting directors find to be very attractive when considering talent for whatever new project of theirs just got the green light. Trust me. I have experience. I have knowledge. I pick up the phone and people have no choice but to do exactly what it is I tell them to do. Because, and it's very simple, because they have not been around the block so they do not recognize a big fat hosing when it walks up and introduces itself, and I do. You want him here? Fine. I said fine. You wanna do this show? Fine. But there are things you cannot say, and I wanna make sure that that is made absolutely crystal clear. Is it?

Dramatic
Maddie, early to mid-thirties

MADDIE: Have either of you ever been a witness to the actions of a gang or a mob? No? Then imagine for the moment that you're a sixteen year old girl. Five foot three, ninety-five pounds. You're good in school, but you can't be too good because guys don't like girls that are smart, or at least just not girls that are smarter than they are. You work a job after school to help save money to pay for your college books and tuition. You have a boyfriend that loves you, but has begun pressuring you to be more physically intimate with him. Your family is Roman Catholic. You've always been taught that God won't love you if you have sex before you're married, that your parents won't love you if you have sex before you're married, that no one will love you if you have sex before you're married. You will be cast out of the village for committing the crime of having pre-marital sex. But at the same time you love your boyfriend, and you know that he loves you. You want to be more physically intimate. You ask yourself, who am I hurting, in the end, who am I hurting if my boyfriend and I are more physically intimate with each other? So, one night, you agree to go out with him in his convertible. He drives you out to a hillside overlooking the town, and there under the cover of starlight and moonlight, the car radio acting as your own personal Maurice Chevalier, you find that you're both each succumbing to your basic human desires. Then you wake up a month later and discover you're pregnant, but it's okay because it's not like your family's that religious, right? No, wait, I misspoke, they're very Roman Catholic. So, what do you do? Well, first you tell your mother, who tells your father, who turns around and decides to rip you a new one. You little whore, he says, how could you have been so unbelievably stupid, how could you have allowed yourself to be taken in by this lying, self-serving, predatory fraction of a man? So, now that you feel like the lowest of the low, after you feel like you've betrayed your parents, your boyfriend, and Jesus Christ himself. Now that all you want to do is go into your room and slit your wrists with a razor, you realize you can't because there's a tiny little organism that has begun to grow inside of you. You are now responsible for what happens to this tiny little organism. You have the option of keeping it, of helping it grow to a full and healthy lifespan. Or you can get rid of it because you're sixteen, you can't support yourself, let alone the needs of a newborn baby, and you want to go to college so you can get a job and move out from under the financial umbrella of your parents so that one day you might be able to do just that, to support the needs of a newborn baby. So, let's say you live in New York or Oregon, two states that do not require parental consent or notification to abort a pregnancy. You drive to the abortion clinic, but when you get there you see a mob of people standing between you and the front door holding signs and shouting things that make you want to turn around and hide under your bed. But you can't. You have to be brave. The problem is, it's hard to be brave when you're five feet three inches and ninety-five pounds. So, very quietly and very slowly you get out of your car. You walk towards the front door of the building, trying hard to avoid the gaze of what feels like a hundred pairs of eyes, all of whom have just decided to make you the new focus of their rage and ignorance. What happens next? From out of nowhere someone's hand slaps you across the face. If you weren't feeling bad enough before, you sure as hell feel like crap now. All you can do is run and hope they don't catch you and rip you to pieces before you can get to the other side of the front door. Why does Congress need to make it illegal to protest outside abortion clinics in this country? Because women seeking abortions shouldn't be made to feel like criminals.

Comic
Lucy, twenty-five, Latina

Lucy is trapped in an apartment with her delusional mother. In this monologue, Lucy finally finds a friend/ potential suitor in Milton, to whom she speaks about her job delivering pizzas and other things she finds interesting and, perhaps, impressive, on their first date.

LUCY: I like my job. Other people might not like it, but I do. I get a kick out of the kids who come up to me with thirty-six cents for a slice. "Don't you know what century this is, kid?" I say. They don't have a clue. So I give it to them anyway. I don't care. Why should I care? They're just little kids . . . You know what else I like? I like it when they turn off the ovens and everybody goes racing home . . . That's when I whip out a bag of Twizzlers—I find licorice real relaxing, you know what I mean? It like gives you time to think because you gotta chew it so long. I come to some interesting ideas that way. I'm gonna write a book about that place someday. One chapter is gonna be just about Twizzlers and the things it makes you think. Another one's gonna be about sex. It's something the way people carry on there. There was this one woman who used to come around all the time. We called her Blowjob Linda; she used to grab guys and take 'em into the toilet with her. They'd come out minutes later with their shirts out and their flies open, looking like something blown in out of a tropical storm. Anyway, that's Linda. I could write a whole chapter just about her. You know what I mean? She had style. Not too many people with that. Yeah . . . you see all types. I think that's why I like it so much. It's always in-ter-esting. I think so anyway. I don't know about anybody else.

(Pause)
You know what else? I like talking people into buying things they don't know they want . . . Yeah, that's the best. Pizza with pineapple and anchovies. Man, some people are sooo stupid, they'll eat anything.

(Pause)
Some people tell me I'm too old to be delivering pizzas, but isn't that who you would want delivering your pizza? Somebody older. Somebody responsible. You know how not getting a pizza you ordered could ruin your evening. You could be left there with nothing to eat. And then you would have to go out. That's what I save people from. From the streets. From seeing other people. From having other people see them. I'm a shield.

Information on this playwright may be found at:
www.smithandkraus.com.
Click on the AUTHORS tab.

LUCY LOVES ME

Migdalia Cruz

Seriocomic
Cookie, forty-five. Latina

Cookie is a faded & desperate former beauty queen. In this monologue, Cookie is talking/ranting to herself, to her neighbors, to her daughter, Lucy—all in Cookie's imagination. Her daughter has just left the house, and Cookie gets to talk about the things she dreams about— like her neighbor Mr. 5K, who bangs on his ceiling when Cookie sings.

COOKIE: I can't stand it here. No one could. I hate her and I hate this room and I hate my life . . . I don't know why I called her Lucy. That's my name. Everyone thought it would be cute. Only boys are juniors, I said. I said it would be dumb. I said it was too pretty a name for such an ugly baby. And-it was ugly. I'm not just saying that. Believe me. I was there. She didn't have any hair on her head until she was five. Ugly. Ugly, I tell you. Plain ugly. That's when I changed my name to Cookie. Who does she think she is anyway? I'll tell you what she is. She's an ugly little girl who's bad to her mother. She doesn't care if our home smells like the monkey house in the zoo . . . I haven't been there in a long time. I don't go anywhere. I don't remember what the Atlantic Ocean looks like . . . It probably hasn't changed though. But I'd like to see it again anyway . . . She likes the way it smells. She likes everything rotten. Her food tastes rotten. I can't even get a decent piece of cheese around here. One side or the other always has something green on it. She just cuts it off, but me, I can't do that—that's the kind of hairpin I am. I think he robs banks.

(Pause)

Mr. 5K robs banks. Small ones and he keeps the loot stashed in his ceiling under a drop tile. I wonder if he'd murder me if he knew I knew his secret. I won't tell anyone though, Mr. 5K. I don't snitch. There's honor here. And I'm full of it.

(singing)

"Oh, beautiful, for spacious skies . . . " He loves it when I sing . . . Hey, Mister 5K do you play on your piccolo when I sing? I bet you do. I bet you beat your tom-tom for Cookie-Lucy . . . I coulda done it professionally, know what I mean? I used to always go around singing to myself, and people—people I didn't even know—would come up to me and ask if I was a pro. It's something the way people pick up on the truth like that. I mean, I wasn't a singer but that's what I always wanted to be. And people just pick that stuff right up, just like that . . . It's funny, isn't it? I mean, you never know. People always surprise you.

Information on this playwright may be found at:
www.smithandkraus.com.
Click on the AUTHORS tab.

Dramatic
Rita, late sixties

Rita's husband Ben is dying of cancer. Her daughter is a divorced not-so-recovering alcoholic and her son is a writer who never writes anything and who has an imaginary boyfriend. Ben lies in a hospital bed, heavily sedated. She addresses this to him while he's sleeping.

RITA: Ben. Our children are a disaster. Lonely and terrible . . . . I blame you . . . . Of course, I was there. So I can't, in all fairness, lay all the debris at your feet. I was there. I watched. I watched it all, and I remember everything. I do. I remember the first time I saw you. I was with a friend, we were so young, and you walked over to the car and the sun was behind you so I couldn't see your face. But as soon as I did. I could see, right then, that first moment, that you loved me . . . And I was trapped. And I tried, for a very long time and with all my might, to love you back. I remember the very first time you ever touched me . . . I remember sitting, by myself, in the dark, in the middle of the night. I remember your face, so dark and hard, like metal. And although I've tried, I *don't* remember, when it happened, the moment when I started hating you. I've searched and searched. I've looked in every corner, but I can't find it. I suppose it isn't really there. No moment. No single second when it happened. It was slow and inevitable, like getting old. I didn't hear it happen, and then I noticed that it had. It had to. And all you ever did was love someone you thought I was . . . And now you get to leave . . . . And I am . . . so frightened. You've been my work for all these years. And I have never been alone.

(She starts to cry.)
I don't know what to do, or what I am.

Information on this playwright may be found at:
www.smithandkraus.com.
Click on the AUTHORS tab.

Dramatic
Rita, late sixties

Rita is the matriarch of a very dysfunctional family. Her daughter is a divorced not-so-recovering alcoholic, her son is a writer who never writes anything and her husband Ben, with whom she had an extremely contentious relationship, has just died of cancer. Here, she tells her children that she is running off with a much younger man to start a new life. They have asked her why she would do such a thing.

RITA : *(triumphant)* BECAUSE I CAN! Because I have to! I think I have to! There is nothing for me here. Yes, to the naked eye, there are connections. I have children. I have friends. But my friends are strangers and my children are sad and unforgiving. Lisa, I cannot live, every day, under the mountain of tragedy you create. Your life is too treacherous and too exhausting. A cloud passes in front of the sun and you see Armageddon! Curtis, whatever your childhood was, it's an old book and the pages are faded. You refuse to forgive anyone for anything and it's enough! I realize you are who you are and I bear responsibility. But the days turn into years and it has to end! I'm doing this because I spent forty years in a marriage to a man I never loved. But even contempt is a connection—and now that's gone and I am rootless in the world. I'm doing this because I'm still alive and I have to find a way to try to feel *something!* It may seem fast, or look abrupt, but that's the way the world is. You wait and wait and wait and then everything changes, all at once! And yes, I'm scared. I am scared to death. But I'm going to take this leap. Do you understand me?! I want to spend my time on the sand, in the sun, by the water, with a man too young for me, because I'm in a position to it! Do I love him? No. Does he love me? I doubt it very much. But he's nice. And he thinks I'm funny and we aren't locked in some war that never ends! I'm sorry if you feel abandoned, but you're adults now and it's time. It's past time! Your father is gone and I *have* to become something else! Raymond is waiting for me and we are going to Aruba. Tonight! I'm going to fly away from this place and you and my life! I'm going to start over, all over! I am leaving! And you can shout bon voyage, or, frankly, you *can both go fuck yourselves!*

Information on this playwright may be found at:
www.smithandkraus.com.
Click on the AUTHORS tab.

Seriocomic
Sarah, twenty-two

Sarah is addressing her kindergarten class.

SARAH: Okay, has everyone found their own space? Make sure you're not touching anyone else. Not with your feet. Hey. Not with your feet. Touching includes your feet. Now close your eyes. It's okay if you forget the things I'm about to tell you. A long time ago, there was a medieval festival called Samhain in a country called Ireland. This festival marked the end of the harvest. Harvest is when farmers would go collect all the crops they grew and pick them and sell them or eat them or store them before the winter. This festival signaled the end to the lighter part of the year and the beginning of the darker part of the year. People would make huge bonfires and remember the dead. People would gather with their livestock and tell stories about their ancestors. An ancestor is the person in your family you came from, who came before you. A parent. A grandparent. A great grandparent. And after the people told stories about their ancestors, they would throw the bones of their slaughtered livestock into the bonfires. And now, instead of doing that, we celebrate Halloween. Hey. I see some feet touching some other feet. I'm not going to say it again. Everyone gets their own space. Okay? *(She smiles)* Hey, eyes closed. Now. Everyone rest for five more minutes. We have five minutes to close our eyes before we line up for the parade. Close your eyes Puppy. Close your eyes fairy princess I'm sorry, regular princess. No touching. Eyes closed.

Information on this playwright may be found at:
www.smithandkraus.com.
Click on the AUTHORS tab.

THE MAN UNDER
Paul Bomba

Dramatic
Lisa, twenty-six

*Lisa is talking to Jeff. She is a strange woman who likes to
jump on the subway track and lay down flat while a train
passes over her.*

LISA: Well, I had a fantasy too. I dreamt of throwing myself
on the tracks. And once I was with you, but you were
some other guy with some other problem and he also
looked into my eyes as he grabbed that pole. I reached out
for him and he slipped away and took the leap. That leap
that I've been somehow fucking preventing myself from
taking for the last eight, nine years. It's in slow motion,
the way he moved . . . This hauntingly beautiful dance
where the soul vacates the body and a powerful negative
force propels this empty, mobile husk. One step and . . .
I tried not to watch . . . but I was compelled to. Coerced
by those tortured green eyes that spoke wordless to me
not six seconds before. Just that one step and he seemed
to . . . to just float there, balanced in the air for just this
hair of a time. Just long enough for me to see a flash—a
flash of regret in his eyes. He was looking at me asking
me why I wasn't ready to save him, and I didn't have
the answer. I could only stare into the depths of someone
who was making that most permanent mistake. And I just
. . . Time starts again and there's a terrible sound, the train
grinds to a screeching halt, and the conductor runs out,
yelling "MAN UNDER MAN UNDER MAN UNDER!"
like him shouting louder and louder was gonna raise the
dead. The blood was splattered all over the platform and
I started to hate that . . . I could've helped. Reached out.
But I was only able to watch as a horror unfolded in real
time right in front of me . . . With those green eyes . . .

After a moment, I reached down for this . . .

(Takes off glove.)

The other one, well, it was down there on the tracks, probably mangled and broken like the rest of him. But this was saved, and it fell at my feet, like some kind of offering. The damnedest things happen when the human body is obliterated at high speeds . . . Physics, you know? Gloves come off.

(pause)

So that's it, now you know. And now you know why I needed to save you, see? You'll never be the man under. I won't let it happen. Because I'm loving you and holding on. And we'll never be able to regret anything. Because we're in some kind of . . . Some kind . . . of love.

Information on this playwright may be found at:
www.smithandkraus.com.
Click on the AUTHORS tab.

Comic
Effie, late twenties

Effie approaches a handsome stranger in a bar

EFFIE: So studies show that the of all the countries in the world American women are some of the worst at flirting. Or, like, approaching men, initiating contact, whatever. I didn't actually read the study but I read about it online, I'm not really in the habit of reading scientific studies, I mean, maybe I should be, maybe that's like what's wrong with my life but this study totally supports the argument that gender roles are culturally taught and are not biologically innate, which I totally believe. But it's really hard to go against years and years of cultural programing that aggressive women are easy and no one wants to marry the slut and that men enjoy the chase and you should play hard to get otherwise its boring. As though men are cats with a piece of string. And I realize that's not really a metaphor that makes sense but whatever. Simile? Metaphor. Whatever. But just because something is hard doesn't mean you shouldn't work on it. Being good at being aggressive, I mean, generally speaking, not just, like, flirting. And I am trying. I'm getting better. I asked for a raise at work, finally, I should have asked for it like six months ago, and it was awful and horrible and goes against my nature both because I want everyone to like me but also because I'm not really sure I'm worth twelve dollars an hour, you know? But I did it and even though I thought I was going to vomit it actually ended up really awesome. I mean I didn't get what I asked for but I did get a raise and that's good right? I mean, I'm half Jewish so you'd think I'd be good at negotiating but I'm really really not. When I bought my car I got so ripped off and

I knew it but I didn't say anything because I was embarrassed. Is that anti-Semitic? Is something still racism even if its positive? Like saying mixed race babies are cuter? Am I allowed to say that? Because it's true, you know. But what I was saying is that I'm working on it, being aggressive, or well not aggressive but like stating what I want and feeling entitled that I deserve what I want and anyway I think you're sort of cute. Well not sort of cute, actually cute. You are actually cute. And so I'm trying to do this thing where if I think someone is cute I go up and tell them and this is really terrifying and I would like to buy you a beer if you want or if you don't want you can take the compliment because it's true that you're cute and if you want a beer I will be sitting over there and oh my god I am so sorry I will leave.

THE MISSIONARY POSITION
Keith Reddin

Dramatic
Julie, forties

Julie, a wealthy socialite who dreams of holding office, is a woman of great entitlement and self-involvement, but she has limited taste and less patience. She has been drafted by a political campaign to lend her money and support with the promise of a future appointment.

JULIE: You said yourself we need to overcome our personal feelings, feelings of animosity, and focus on the good we're doing. Just the other day I was campaigning for Williams, and I make it a point to make contact with the people. I stopped in this one town, about an hour and a half south of the state capitol and I took part in a spaghetti dinner at the VFW hall there. It was a wonderful event and there was a really nice crowd of supporters there, maybe fifteen senior citizens, they asked some very tough questions, but towards the end of the night I found myself alone with a young college student. This young man was studying accounting at the local college and we were talking and at some point we realized that everybody else had sort of drifted away. And this young man, his name was Terry, he was very bright, he asked me all sorts of provocative questions about tax codes and I noticed we were sitting very close. Our chairs were next to each other, and our knees were sort of touching, and I have to say, that I have very attractive legs, I mean I exercise every day and I swim whenever I get the chance in my pool, and my legs, well they're, firm, very firm and muscular, but not in a lesbian tennis player sort of way, shapely, and we looked at each other, and Terry has a skin condition which with the proper help could be cleared up in no time, but he's sort of cute, very young and earnest, and I knew on some deep level, beyond all the talk about repeal of estate taxes, we had connected. I had reached him. And I knew that that was more important than anything else. That for every angry non believer who tries to run me over, I can affect someone else who believes in what I believe in. And that gave me great strength. And what I'm trying to remind you of what you tell me all the time, to rise above and have faith that we will, you know, in the end, prevail.

Dramatic
Gina, thirties

Gina owns a bar frequented by college students. She is talking to Milo, a campus security guard who hangs out there.

GINA: Well it looks like there might be some people interested in buying the bar. Those guys back there from the City? We've been talking for a couple of weeks. Technically I'm not supposed to say anything yet—but they just walked right in here the other day and made me an offer. I mean I guess every other place around here near the Hudson is getting bought and refurbished. Anyway I just want to take my money and get out of this dump. It's just . . . I've been here too long, y'know? It's like you begin to notice things like how the only clear radio station plays the same 9 oldie songs over and over again and how the only people around here are either college kids or trust-fund hippies, or . . . sports-obsessed meatheads.

> *(Beat.)*

And I don't like the nights here. It's like, growing up around here I was always scared of the wind at night, y'know? There's such a particular howl it has. And it used to remind me of like ghosts and werewolves and, I don't know, just horror movie stuff. But then as I grew up, it started reminding me of other things. Much scarier things. Like . . . growing old I guess. And being alone. Just totally completely alone where you go out during the day and shop for groceries just so you can eat them by yourself at night while you watch these TV shows that are filled with images of a world you don't even belong to. But that you convince yourself you *do*. And you keep trying to remember what it was like to be there, cause you can't face the fact that you're totally isolated. Alienated from everything and just completely alone. And you just keep on passing the time, passively passing time. Until you're old. And your bones won't move. And then that's it, there's nothing left. There's just—and you never even . . .

(She gets choked up. She takes a deep breath.)

Sorry. Maybe I'm crazy. I just don't want to hear that howl anymore y'know? I wanna go someplace warm, where the sun sets late, and there are lots of people around and I don't have to drive all the time and I just never want to hear that howl again.

Information on this playwright may be found at: www.smithandkraus.com. Click on the AUTHORS tab.

Dramatic
Ginny, mid to late thirties

*Ginny is a porn star who acts under the name "Osprey
Hepburn." She is speaking to Robert, who has stumbled
onto the set of one of her films being shot and who knows
nothing about the porn business. He has asked her how
she got into porn.*

GINNY: I fell in love with one asshole after another and
wound up dropping out of college my sophomore year
and marrying the biggest asshole of the lot. I still
don't know why. The people he hung out with—
scum of the earth. But, at the same time, I found I
could play them, you know? I guess I got off on it
at first. It was easier than college. So, I worked the
graveyard shift at a diner while Prince Charming
sat on his ass and partied. Well, he went from bad
to worse. He started squandering what little money
we had. He lost what I laughingly refer to as his job.
Then he just got lost, period, leaving me holding the
bag. Not only for the bills, but for his extracurricular
activities as well—by the end, he was hanging out
with a whole new class of scumbag and getting his
drugs from people who can't be played so easily.
Well, after a year or so of doing not so nice things
to keep the wolves at bay and maintain a roof over
my head, I had learned one hell of a lot about the
way the world really works. Then one of his quote-
unquote "business associates" was encouraged by
law enforcement to relocate. He wound up buying a
strip club in St. Louis and I worked out a deal with

him. And that, I believe, is where we came into the movie. My path opened up for me. I met Peter, moved here to the Valley, and for a lot of years I was happy. Or so I thought. It was exciting, too. Being the center of attention. It was liberating. The sad truth is that people outside the industry want nothing to do with you once they know what you are, but they'll go home to their computers and jerk off to you all night. Osprey Hepburn is a carry-on goodie bag. Ginny Ryan requires at least two claim tickets and a fork lift. When your business is sex, you renounce intimacy. Forever. Sex is all around you, but intimacy—good luck finding it. When I was in high school I read a book about this prostitute. She'd do anything sexually, no matter how disgusting—but she wouldn't kiss. I never understood that. Until I got into the business. Ah, we're all in prison. I just happen to be in solitary. I don't even remember what the sky looks like. I'd give anything to have a real conversation with someone. To kiss a man for real.

Information on this playwright may be found at:
www.smithandkraus.com.
Click on the AUTHORS tab.

NEVA

Guillermo Calderón. English translation by Andrea Thome

Dramatic
Masha, thirty-six

*The actress Olga Knipper, Chekhov's widow, has asked
Masha and Aleko, two actors in her company, to act out
the scene when Chekhov told his sister, with whom he was
living, that he intended to marry Olga.*

MASHA: That fat pig, that old, crosseyed, crippled, hunch-
backed Olga Knipper, unfashionable, broken puppet of
Nemirovich-Danchenko and Stanislavsky, hen, hillbilly,
gravedigger. I hate her. Actress, criminal, when she stands
up on stage it stinks like a lion. Anton, Antosha: Why did
we grow up? We were so happy when we were little and
we played in the mud. I want to be little again Anton.
Choose me, I know you from before. You know what
I want? I want you to marry her, to write plays for her
and make her into a goddess, and to keep her far away,
in Moscow, and to cry over her absence. And to cough
more each day, and to realize that the one who stayed
by your side until the end was me, and that the sex and
nasty things that you wanted so badly didn't mean a
thing. And for you to die one day, and for her to suffer,
drowning in guilt, and for her to get fat, so she can't act
anymore. And I'm going to stay in this house and I'm
going to leave everything untouched until it becomes a
museum. I'm going to become a selfish giant and your
orchard will dry up. *Oh, my dear, my sweet, my beautiful
orchard . . .*

  (to Olga)
Swine, vile German, you managed to trap my brother. If
you become Natasha from *Three Sisters*, I will strangle
you with my own hands. I won't bite your throat, I'll

just strangle you . . . I want to kill myself, my life has no meaning anymore . . . all because of my brother's marriage . . . Why did Olga have to bother, and complicate everything for a sick man? It's so strange that you're going to become a Chekhova. Olga, Olechka, you know I adore you . . . I've become so close to you over the last two years . . . Please, find me a rich and generous boyfriend.

Information on this playwright may be found at:
www.smithandkraus.com.
Click on the AUTHORS tab.

Lawrence Harbison

THE NORWEGIANS
C. Denby Swanson

Comic
Betty, twenties to thirties

Betty, a transplant from Kentucky, has lived in Minnesota for five long winters. Her heart has recently been broken by a Minnesota man of Norwegian descent.

You could do this as direct address to the audience, or she could be talking to another woman she's met in a bar.

BETTY: The Norwegians. They are insidious. Dangerous. Clever. Strong. They are weather proofed, as children, to not mind extreme cold or large flying bugs. Or Canada. They don't mind being close to Canada. They are insulated, somehow. Well trained for outdoor survival. Even babies. They kayak. Babies! Yes. They ski. It is like they are all little baby Navy SEALS. They learn to drive on frozen rivers, they learn how to slam on the brakes and spin wildly into the snow. Not babies. But teenagers. And on purpose, not like the rest of us, as an act of rebellion, or inadvertently because we don't know how to brake, but sanctioned, organized, they are trained to do it the right way. All their driver education classes take place outside in the winter on frozen rivers. All of them. On purpose. Training little Norwegian Jason Bournes. They are well fed, despite the limited window for agriculture, but they rarely get fat. In fact, they appear wholesome. And charming. And handsome. And perfect. And pure. But they're not. Don't be fooled. They prioritize social services, like elder care—they even call it *elder care*—and drug rehab for teenagers and independent living programs for the mentally ill—and they give to the arts with an unshakeable ferocity, even in difficult economic times, even in deficit years, as if they actually believe in those things, in the worth of those things, in the benefits of community. I asked one, I asked why, why these donations, why all this money going to artists and addicts and museums and public gardens? And he said, Because otherwise it would be like living in Omaha, only further north. I swear, it's what he said directly to me. Asshole. Think they're loyal, upstanding citizens? Think again. Norwegians started colonizing this country five centuries before Columbus. Greedy bastards. Never in large numbers. Secretly. Under the radar. Until they dominated the lumber trade and farming and fishing and crafts trades and back home there was a crisis and they decided to take over the flat, fertile land of our precious Midwest. Like they take over our flat, fertile women. There are five million of them now, in this country, committed to their homes and parks and neighborhood watch groups and to their extended families, too. "Family," right? You've seen *The Godfather*. But note this: In the last hundred years, almost no Norwegians have become Mormon. Okay? Right? You don't find that suspicious? Who can resist the Mormons these days? They knock on the doors of Jehovah's Witnesses and walk away with new converts. I mean, Mormons are freaking everywhere, and they have that pitch about saving the souls of your dead relatives, despite the fact that they're *dead*, if their souls are anywhere they're in Hell, you can imagine your great aunt suddenly yanked out of the fire, Oh, she says as the flames recede, I knew I could count on that one, my niece, she is such a nice person. But Norwegians, no. They're like, Well, now there's a hot dish, oh sure. I'm telling you, a practical people. Warm. Thoughtful. Destructive. Evil. Don't ever fall in love with one of them.

Information on this playwright may be found at:
www.smithandkraus.com.
Click on the AUTHORS tab.

Lawrence Harbison

Comic
Betty, twenties to thirties

At a bar at happy hour, Betty advises her new friend Olive about the challenge of boyfriend hunting in a place like Minnesota.

BETTY: Here in Minnesota, you gotta find a lover before the first freeze or else it's just too late, you're iced in for a very long time, all alone. They don't tell you that when you move here but it's true. You are iced in for all the short days, there are so many short days before the sun comes back and it begins to thaw. Short days and long nights. Long cold nights all alone, just the sound of the radiator in your apartment turning on, the knocking and the whispering of steam. Just leftover soup heated up mid-afternoon before the light fades. In fact, you make so much borscht that your poop turns red and you think it's blood and you have to have a tube with a camera on it shoved up your ass. On camera. In February. And the doctor aims the tube at you and says, "Here we go!" and then you watch your looming butt cheeks docked like the international space station by a tiny camera on a tube, like the space shuttle, right there on TV. It's that kind of cold, Olive. It's the cold of those bulky purple and yellow sweaters that you have to put on to take out the garbage, so that you're shapeless, like a big purple and yellow potato. That's you: a big plate of starch. You're just purple and yellow and shapeless and starchy, and you've just had a camera up your ass. Unless of course you find a lover, and hold on to him, and you make your own steam, and knocking, and whispering, and you feed each other food from your hands, not soup but solid food, and you draw lines with ice cubes down each other's body, no one's cold then. No one's cold. No one's alone. So did you do that, Olive? Did you find someone before it froze? No. Oh, you tried, now, didn't you. But you failed. You didn't get a lover. No. No, you didn't. Because he left you. He froze you out. He left you to die. *That* is Minnesota nice, my new little friend. What I just did to you. That's what Minnesota nice feels like in your heart after five years. Five winters. That's all it takes. Unless of course you were raised here. Which I wasn't. I am from Kentucky.

Information on this playwright may be found at:
www.smithandkraus.com.
Click on the AUTHORS tab.

Comic
Betty, twenties to thirties

Betty and her new friend Olive are commiserating over their recent traumatic breakups. Olive believes in astrology but Betty thinks it's a crock.

BETTY: Here's a reason the astrology column was always in the section of the newspaper with the comic strips and the weird little narratives about bridge games. Or the back of the magazine. Or the add-on to Facebook, like Farmville, or what, like what, like some stupid little app. But you take it seriously? Seriously? You take it seriously? You're one of those people? You, like, have an actual, like you have a person that you call? Jesus. Did your astrologer tell you that an awful man you loved was going to break your heart? Did she tell you, don't go to the fancy Italian restaurant that he yelped and got all excited about, because it's a set up? Because you will be ambushed? Did she happen to mention that your boyfriend is a fucking power hungry fucking asshole, by the way, clue number one is that he picked someplace special and expensive so that you won't scream and cry—he thinks you might, by the way, and he thinks he's being *nice* when he—when he pulls the plug and leaves you there to gasp for air and die. Weren't you wondering, sitting like a dumb ass, not breathing, not moving, as he says what he says, watching the truck come at you, bam! There's a $45 entrée and another glass of wine on its way, he says, graciously, get whatever you want, it's on me, and you don't wonder why you hadn't been warned by your FUCKING ASTROLOGER? Instead you quietly sob with your head in your hands and people stare but you don't make a sound. Do you think your ex just had a better planetin his house that day than you?

Information on this playwright may be found at:
www.smithandkraus.com.
Click on the AUTHORS tab.

Comic
Betty, twenties to thirties

Betty has befriended Olive in a Minnesota bar at happy hour. But neither of them is very happy. Olive's boyfriend recently dumped her and Betty is furious with the local Norwegians.

BETTY: The Norwegians. And their Lutheran Church. Home of orphan and refugee relocation services all over the world. Their revered social services. Fuck me. Fuck them. The Norwegians and their *gravlaks*. Does anyone even know what that is? An alien word for, I don't know, something fishlike. And fermented trout. Fermented. Trout. And *lutefisk*—fish steeped in lye and then covered in ashes. I mean, my god, fish, lye and ashes. Fish, Lye & Ashes. It sounds like a band name from the 1970's. Like, a white R &B band. And their perpetually cheerful snow suits and their stupid local customs. They will stop in any weather and help a stranger change their tire. I just want to scream at them, I know you don't really mean that. You cannot love people who make *gravlaks*. You cannot love people who make *lutefisk*. You cannot FUCK people who make elderberry wine, not an actual fuck, not a true heartfelt beautiful intimate fuck, as I discovered. Late. Or lingonberries. *Lingonberries*. If that doesn't bring up dirty images in your head, I don't know what would. What lover would let you serve them lingonberries? And my god, hotdish: meat and Stovetop drenched in mushroom soup and covered in tater tots. That's not even—that's like casserole death. But Norwegians hand this "food" out in the neighborhood when new people move in. When there are pot lucks. They think hotdish is welcoming. They think lingonberries are—Well. These are fearful, terrifying, terrible, very frightening things to serve people.

Information on this playwright may be found at:
www.smithandkraus.com.
Click on the AUTHORS tab.

Lawrence Harbison

OPEN UP
Kimberly Pau

Dramatic
Medusa, ageless mythical creature

This is direct address to the audience. Medusa serves as a conscience figure for Dwayne. the protagonist of Open Up. She is both an agent of death and a woman desperate to stop other women from being abused and killed as she was.

MEDUSA: I'm just here to do my job. My damn job.
   Do you think someone like me should have to be working?
   I will not be silent. I said I will not be silent!!
   I demand that you hear me speak.
   You can't turn me away.
   You might try.
   I dare you!
   I am the one with a deadly stare and mysterious hair.
   In Africa I am worshipped by the Libyan Amazons as their Serpent Goddess.
   My gross image is represented on the Sicilian flag.
   And yes, I sleep with a knife under my pillow.
   It's a machete!
   Fuck Athena the man-lover.
   I symbolize female mysteries and creativity
   also destruction.
   I have been in punishment for centuries.
   It's ill-suited.
   Completely unfair.
   I am a Gorgon.
   A monster.
   Virile. Charming. Evil. Witchy. Lost in the abyss.
   Terrifying.

HISS!
I don't want to answer to you.
I want to answer to no one.
There is one element of my task that I admire, however.
Like
a snake that constantly sheds and renews its skin.
I have the ability to create and annihilate life.
Annihilate.
Annihilate.

Dramatic
Belleesha, forty-three, Latina

Belleesha gives a drunken eulogy at the funeral of her best friend, Tiny Marie, who has died in a fire started by her 3 year-old son, Dwayne. Belleesha has been granted custody of Dwayne, who is also a successful emerging pop star.

BELLEESHA: It comes with a big burden. A big big big big burden. I mean being a new mom. Even though I was Dwayne's godmother before, since before he was born even. I was ass kicking for that little fucker, ooo, sorry. But now he is strictly my burden, or responsibility and I am really fine with it. Thrilled I mean. He's not here is he? No. Right, he's with a nanny. The poor girl. I have to pay them triple. Don't fault me for having a few cocktails. I mean, we tried to do this in the Catholic Church but they were like no way! I think this church is Unitarian and they don't give a fuck. I mean, a damn. I mean, they're not gonna pop a nut or nothing. Foof.
  (Sips her drink.)
Long Island Ice Tea has always been my drink. And you know when they say—"that girl can drink," I mean, they say that. Often. But I should be speaking about Marie. Now that she's dead I can say. She was afraid of the baby. Right before she gave birth, when he was still in the womb, she felt him biting, before he had teeth even. Gumming at her insides like a little snapping turtle in her belly. She never had any talent, couldn't hold a tune to save her life but with that baby inside her, she was convinced he was gonna be a big star. But there's definitely something wrong with him. Oh well, he's only 3. So who knows?

(sip)

If I'm the best choice a child's got then that is a very sad thing. Must have been my maternal instinct that kicked in when the house set on fire. It was an absolute mess. People were on fire. Our things. The microwave blew up and the whole downstairs went boom. Mom was wearing something very flammable and whale sized and that went boom. Marie was screaming bloody murder and Dad was in shock so it was my duty to grab the baby and I promise I wasn't even seeing dollar signs. He was biting my poor hand the whole way down the escape rope I made out of the shower curtain. That little shit. I have a scar! It was really just some kind of mother's instinct that I've kept deeply buried until now. But there you go, it's irony! And now I have the dollars and the problems. Can someone bring me another drink up here?

THE OTHER PLACE
Sharr White

Dramatic
Juliana, fifty-two

*Juliana is a scientist who has developed a new drug to
control the onset of dementia. Ironically, she herself has
the disease. She is speaking at a conference. The girl in the
yellow string bikini is her daughter at a very young age.
Her daughter disappeared when she was a teenager.*

JULIANA: Gentlemen. Right now. In here. A new version of
Identamyl is, we're certain, hard at work. Though neuron
death is still occurring, our hope, however, is that it is
slowing, or even coming to a halt.

Regardless of treatment, the memories I had will never be
restored. Neither will my very sense of self, but honestly
who am I really if The Great Darkness as I've begun
referring to it started descending five years ago? Or ten.
Or longer. Not being myself is, oddly, who I am. Very
rarely, triggered by who knows what, visions—ghosts
really—of my past life *do* appear quite vividly. But most
often I must settle for memories of *pictures*. Or memories
of someone telling me . . . of *their* memories . . . of me.
I'm also taking a new drug meant to help *clear* these
plaques, but because it's made by a competitor, if you
ask me what it is . . . I'll tell you I don't remember.

I conclude my lecture. There is applause. There are
many conversations I do not retain. I dine quietly with
Ian in our room, only dimly realizing this has long been
a pleasure of mine. The sun begins to lower. I change
into my swimsuit again and descend, unassisted, into the
pool. I float. I breathe. I am a woman in-between: The

sky and the earth. The past and the future. This place
. . . and the other.

And then it happens. The water flattens. The sky reddens.
The breeze stills. The earth turns. And the girl in the yellow string bikini . . . comes back to me.

Information on this playwright may be found at:
www.smithandkraus.com.
Click on the AUTHORS tab.

OUTLOOK
Kathleen Warnock

Dramatic
Patience, late thirties

Patience, a Certified Financial Planner. Her girlfriend Susan has asked her what they mean to each other.

PATIENCE: I really don't like it when people ask me to do things I'm not good at. Like talk about my . . . what we . . . I thought you understood that. I'm smart. I'm very, very smart. That is what I *have*, Susan. I like to think of my brain as a sort of glorious umbrella, covering and protecting everything in my world. I imagine the tendrils of my thoughts, like a filigree, or an exquisitely detailed chandelier, a hierarchy of logic and intelligence, and dare I say wisdom, reaching up and out, and giving light and shelter, and making a logic that serves as a structure for all that I accomplish in my life. It's a pristine equation, the product of a lifetime of hard work and good intentions, and an intellect to be proud of, one to burnish and cultivate as it glistens with the high polish of civilization. I am, you know. Civilized. And I look at you, and suddenly my center is located much to the south, and I lose my discretion, and my grandiloquence, and all I can think of is feelings, and desires, and what was glittering, impenetrable crystal becomes hot and soft, waves of feeling, rather than thought, and what I want seems much more simple and direct: bite, lick, suck, kiss, hold, squeeze, touch, taste, lick, grasp, groan, take, join, give, fall, quake, pull, cry, kneel, call, need, want, come. You open your house . . . open your heart . . . next thing you know, she's taking the pictures off the walls. Taking the covers in bed at night, emptying the joint account. I don't have nearly as much as you think, Susan. I'm not a rich woman.

Dramatic
Susan, mid-forties

Susan, a corporate trainer, comes home a little tipsy. She's worried about being laid off. She's talking to her lover, Patience, and her daughter, Ella.

SUSAN: . . . I had a glass of wine. And a beer. And a Long Island Iced Tea at a bar on the corner. And the bartender bought me another one. WHERE ARE MY GODDAM KEYS? *(She dumps her bag out)* It's not like we're all great FRIENDS, or anything . . . but we're COLLEAGUES. You get to care. See them in the elevator, chat in the break room. They have kids. They have families. They knit. Then they're laid off, took a buyout, if they were lucky. You walk the departments, see the boxes by the cubes. They leave those cardboard sheets that fold into boxes at your desk. You see them when you come in. You check your email, and it says to report to Human Resources. If they worry about you, they have you escorted out. They take your ID. And when it happens, you see heads popping up over the walls of the cube farm, as you do the walk of shame, and people won't look at you . . . and they update their resumes, and email their friends to see if anyone else is hiring. I didn't lose it yet. Not this round. But the plague has begun. A few empty offices today. More next week. The janitors roam up and down the cubes, yelling "bring out your dead." I don't feel redundant.
    (Pause)
I keep thinking there needs to be more light in here . . . or maybe I'm mixing it up with joy. Well, the days are getting longer. Soon we'll be able to walk around without our coats. Feel a breeze of fresh air that doesn't chill you to the bone.

Dramatic

Lavinia, twenties, African American

A mysterious man has just informed Lavinia that she will never see him again, then lovingly injected her with heroin. Lavinia speaks as the drug overtakes her.

LAVINIA: Time machines. This scientist invented a machine that makes people go back in time. But the thing was the person would get younger if they went back. And older if they went forward. It was a great invention but you could only travel in your lifetime. The writing was cheesy and all over the place but I liked the ideas in it. And then . . . then . . . then I took my husband by the hand, I took Leon by the hand and we kissed and I could still smell the saliva on my skin. I always like that. The smell of his saliva on my skin. And he put a rose in my hair. A fire rose like red and orange and I'd never seen it before, never seen a rose that color anywhere in my life and we went in the machine. We went in that machine that makes time go forward and backward. But we didn't go in it. We didn't step in it. It just happened. We went about our lives and the machine did whatever it did to make whatever it did happen. Oh God oh God am I losing my mind? I can't tell if I'm losing my mind but no, no I'm not. He's here. He's right beside me right now and we're getting younger. And I move out of the apartment and take back all my things and gradually we fall out of love, we forget we love each other really slow but it's nice because I see him for the first time, the last time I'll see him again for the first time in his suit back stage and it dies within me, that feeling dies and his smile fades from his face and then we're just two people again. We're two people standing side by side with nothing to say to one another. And that's where it stops. Two people. And the rose he gave me is just a seed curled in my ear waiting to die.

Dramatic
Sheri, mid-thirties

Sheri is speaking to Musa, a taxi driver, who's invited her back to his apartment after her night shift as a waitress has ended. There's a sexual charge and flirtation going on between them.

SHERI: Yeah, I am being followed. [By] you. And before you, everything else that's after me. All the stuff I should be dealing with but avoid. And you know—somehow—the mess I'm trying to avoid, usually finds its way back into my life in the shape of a guy. Like almost always, actually. It's been weirdly predictable. So that—whatever guy I find somehow ends up like—embodying the very things I don't want to deal with. A sort of karmic synchronicity I call it. Like if I've been particularly bad about paying my bills, I'll find a guy who doesn't know how to open up. Give of himself. Like I've found someone who's emotionally stingy. Or else the guy will end up throwing in my face everything I feel bad about because I've usually told him my life story in the first five minutes of meeting him. This has led to some terrific fights. Where the police have been called in. On two occasions I only knew the guys for like forty-eight hours, but somehow managed to crunch six months' worth of going out with someone into that short period. But you know, I think this is why guys are drawn to me, because I'm that accessible. Except when I say accessible, I don't mean easy. Just to put you in the picture, I'm surprisingly on the good girl side of things. Though God knows, I don't hold my liquor well, I mean
  (a laugh; half under her breath)

in about ten minutes I'm going to be a cinch to bang. But just so you know, I'm not the kind of girl who drinks scotch at a stranger's apartment at two am, and all that suggests. I guess that's what I'm trying to say.

Information on this playwright may be found at:
www.smithandkraus.com.
Click on the AUTHORS tab.

Dramatic
Daria, nineteen

Daria is speaking to a self-help group aboard a themed cruise ship that focuses on spiritual ritual. A child of privilege awkwardly searching for her own identity, Daria got her ticket to this cruise as a high school graduation gift from her parents. Daria is addicted to prescription meds and is a self-styled photographer. In this speech, she is trying to explain to a roomful of older adults what she hopes to gain from the mysterious ritual of renewal that is the cruise's main event.

DARIA: Cool
    Um my parents have four
    cars and a massive house
    in a gated community
    That's what I want to find,
    the opposite of—
    Okay
    I've been reading about
    the yaman tribe
    Yammamama.
    And they have rites of
    passage
    When I got my period I
    hid it from my mom and
    she found the tampon
    It was so embarrassing
    Other tribes they have
    rituals for everything but
    not ours.

We don't know how to
connect to our instincts.
My father is fat and
unhappy
I don't want that to be my
life
I want to be able to
connect better with other
people.
Um.
I've been reading about
this guy who talks to this
ape and the ape knows all
these truths
Science tells us that we
need to connect back to
the ape mentality
We build mansions on
native American burial
ground.
We need to get back to
that spirit.
I'm not sure what I'm
talking about.

Dramatic
Esme, eighteen

*Esme has been in a relationship with a much older man,
Fritz. Fritz is a small time thief and full time drunk. In
order to secure her love, Fritz informed on his protégé and
Esme's lover, Jim who was sent to jail as a result. Jim has
recently returned and threatened them both. Fritz tries to
make peace and in explaining his motivation he admits to
Jim that he had a relationship with Esme's Mother. Jim tells
Esme. Esme leaves Fritz. Fritz tries to stop her. Esme, in
frustration, tells Fritz the real reason she is going.*

ESME: Fine. I came. Twice I think. You were drunk so it was
    taking . . . then you made a funny noise and called me
    her name. You called me my Momma's name. You were
    fucked up. Real fucked up. You waited. Waited to see
    if I heard or if I was going to pull away. Leave, call the
    cops or whatever. I didn't know what to do. I was froze
    up. Then all of a sudden you started up again. Hard. Real
    hard. My hips were shaking. Your hand was on my neck.
    Pulling me. Pulling me into you. You said her name again.
    Cried Loraine. Shouted it. I dug in. Started pushing back.
    Me. I wanted to say. It's me. You're fucking me. I was
    angry at first. Then all of a sudden I didn't care. It hurt.
    Hurt nice. Real nice. We went some place and . . . and
    . . . I wanted you to call me Loraine. I wanted you to
    call me every name of every woman you ever dreamed
    of. Fuck it all away. Fuck me faceless. I wanted to be the
    whole goddamned world to you. And I was. I felt I was.
    You came like you was dying. Then slept like you was
    dead. I laid there watchin'. Thinking like a real person

again. Thinking about what it mattered. I said to myself
. . . fuck it. He's mine. I can feel he's mine. I am everything he ever wanted. In his whole life. After tonight I
own him to the bottom. To the toe nail. To the hair on
his knees. His ears will fall off if I tell em. I got him all
and he's got a fair portion of me. After tonight I might
just shave myself bald headed if he asks me. Might just
give him my thumb.

Information on this playwright may be found at:
www.smithandkraus.com.
Click on the AUTHORS tab.

Lawrence Harbison

Seriocomic
May, twenties to thirties

May is a cocktail waitress/bookkeeper in a dive bar in Hollywood. She has been having sex with the bar's owner, Arthur, and is threatening to quit—but not before she gets the money he owes her.

MAY: Oh Arthur, you know me so well, you've finally figured out my heart's desire. After all these years of cheating together you understand what makes me tick. That's right. What I want more than anything in the world is to be treated worse than a dog. More than that, I want to be fucked like a dog and told I'm a dirty little whore and have your fat fingers stuck up me like I'm some kind of clogged pipe. You gonna get me my money, Arthur? So this is what'll happen if I don't get what's mine. I will drive to your little bungalow in Burbank and I will park myself on that fake green lawn of yours and I will get on all fours and pee like a dog on your fucking cactus. And when your nice, fat wife wobbles out I will bark out every mean thing you ever said about her and tell her about our fake plans to open up a clam shack on the beach in Malibu and how it was gonna be called "May's" on account of how you like to yell out my name when you fuck me like a dog. And then I'll apologize to your wife for peeing and barking on her lawn but explain that when someone treats you like a dog long enough, you start to behave like one.

·   *Information on this playwright may be found at:*
www.smithandkraus.com.
Click on the AUTHORS tab.

Dramatic
Leigh, twenty-one

*Leigh's boyfriend/fiancé, Jimmy, has been told that she
had sex at a party with another man. Naturally, he is dev-
astated. Angrily, he has confronted her and here she tells
him what really happened. As the play progresses, though,
we begin to wonder how much of it is true.*

LEIGH: Please. Please, Jimmy. Please. *(Beat)* He wanted to show
me a picture from freshman year, he said. So I went into his
room and I sat on his bed. *(Beat)* He handed me his phone
and told me to find it in there. He came around to look with
me as I flipped through. His face was right next to mine. I
turned to look at him and he kissed me. And I pulled away.
He was drunk, Jimmy, and then . . . He took my hand and he
. . . placed it. There. And I tried to get out of there. I tried to
get Grace, but before I could go his hands were digging into
my shoulders and he just like . . . threw me down, Jimmy.
It was really loud in the other room. I tried to stop him but
his hand was on my face and I just screamed—NO! STOP!
I kept hoping that someone would hear me but I couldn't
breathe in enough air. I couldn't move. I could barely breathe.
I couldn't scream. So I just tried to count down from 200
'cause I figured it'd be over by then. And then—you know—
when he was done. He loosened his hand from around my
neck and I whispered—No—Please. Please, Davis. No. But
it didn't matter. It had happened. And I looked around the
room. And you were out of town. And Grace was out of sight.
And I was alone. Being fucked. So fuck you.

Information on this playwright may be found at:
www.smithandkraus.com.
Click on the AUTHORS tab.

Seriocomic

Rashawn, twenty-one, African American

Rashawn, from Harlem, slipped through the cracks of the NYC foster care system to find herself incarcerated in the NYS penal system. During a surprise visit from her old social worker Anne, Rashawn describes a plate she created in her prison ceramics class.

RASHAWN: I knew what I was doing. And ain't nobody show me, neevah. See, I put that plate back on the spindle. And I start spinnin' it. I put a big ol' glob of burgundy paint in the middle. Then I take my finger and I puuulll the paint to the edge as it's spinning but making these squiggly lines. Then I plop on some bright yellow. I pull it. I put another color, orange, I think. Pull. Another color. Another. And I pull and pull 'til my plate look like a sun- all these colors shooting out the middle? Now it's colorful and all that but I ain't tryna put that shit on nobody wall—it's still a fucking plate. So I put a border around it, you know, to hold all that color? Blue. Cobalt blue, teacher say. And when it dry . . . it was . . . it was . . .

    (Rashawn sees the marvel in her own hands)
And er'body looking . . . Mary. Jeanine. Quanda. Looking. Staring. HATIN'. Cuz it's the best shit goin', kna-mean? Word. So while Mary, Jeanine, Quanda, all them bitches . . . while they looking, staring, hating . . . I just—BLOAW! Pieces of that shit ALL OVER, yo! You shoulda seen motherfuckas faces, yo! Niggas was like, "what the fuck Shawn thinking?! The fuck she doing?" And I'm like, I do cuz I can, nigga! Them bitches could never make no shit like that. They wish.

Seriocomic
Latonya, twenty-five

*Latonya is the young, abrasive mother of Chee-Chee,
a reluctant child genius from the Harlem projects. She
stands behind the counter at her job at Duane Reade and
takes the audience through a day in her life at work.*

LATONYA: E—ver-y where you go-oo . . . da da dada da
da. Duane Reade Reade! Reade! Reade!
Read the fucking signs to find your aisle/yes! I work here
but I ain't gotta smile/no! I told you go to housewares/do
I look like a pharmacist?!/that's a product for hair/no! I
don't want your number/damn! ten minutes til break/a
yo I didn't ring you up, so yo, that ain't my mistake/mis-
ta ojo price check on register four!!!/uh-uh, sir fill that
application out at the back of the store/miss you cain't
return this! You ate the whole damn box/oooh! Rochelle
who's that fine nigga in aisle two wit' the locks?/there's
only one line!!!/damn, my feet straight hurt!!!/we got tic
tacs, take your ass to Rite Aid if you want certs!/we a-bout
to close! Bring all your purchases up!/girl, mista ojo got
me down when I got night school- that's fucked up!/sir I
ain't being rude/you got the fuckin' attitude!/oh no she
didn't come to work wit' them old turn up shoes/who you
tawkin to Rochelle? I know you ain't tryna diss/hold up!/
price check!/this is $3.49, you still want this miss?/price
check!/this is $3.49, you still want this miss?/ hold up!/
price check!/this is $3.49, you still want this miss?/miss
miss miss miss mis-fucking-understood!!!/people stare
at Tonya like I ain't no good/but I ain't rude/ain't got
no attitude/if ya stood in my Gucci boots/ya wouldn't
call me 'rude' hold up!/price check!/this is $3.49, you

still want this miss?/price check!/this is $3.49, you still want this miss?/ hold up!/price check!/this is $3.49, $3.49, $3.49/ ni-ni-ni-ni-ni-ni-ni-ni-nine/nine minutes til break/and I can hardly wait/my son doing homework in the back/I need to make sure he straight/just cause it's noisy here don't mean he can't concentrate/rather that than wit them kids who hate/ aint havin' it/I ain't lettin' him get flipped and kicked by kids acting all jelly and shit/so quick/price check!/this is $3.49, you still want this miss?/price check!/this is $3.49, you still want this miss?/hold up/price check !/ this is $3.49, you still want this miss?/price check!/this is $3.49, you still want this miss? Hold up!

(Sees son.)
CHEE CHEE?!?!

Dramatic
Becky, late teens

*Becky has come to visit her uncle, Sterling, who lives in a
house in the Costa Rican jungle. A girl in her school has
fallen from a window and is in a coma. Becky may have
been responsible, although here she claims she wasn't.*

BECKY: I didn't have anything to do with what happened
to that girl, by the way. My mom doesn't believe me—
she probly told you that. She says she believes me but
I know she doesn't. She thinks I'm lying about like,
every little thing. She thinks what everyone else's parents think—that I'm the one that organized the whole
party and came up with the idea of inviting Slowgirl
and everything. I didn't. I didn't even know there was
gonna be a party until like, the very last minute. I mean,
it wasn't like it was this big, thought-out thing. Jessie's
parents decided *that week* that they were gonna go on a
ski trip up at Stratton, I mean, it's not like we sat down
a month ago and brainstormed it . . . and I didn't even
know they were gonna invite Slowgirl—her real name's
Marybeth, I know it's not a nice nickname but that's what
everyone calls her—I don't want you thinking the whole
time I'm here that I've done something really sick and
awful 'cause I haven't. Plus, I have no idea what my
mom told you so you probly think . . . whatever, I have
no idea what you think. All I did was go to a party just
like pretty much every other junior and senior who has
friends in the whole entire school. It's so fucked up that
I'm pretty much the only one that's, like, in trouble. My
ex-boyfriend Tyler came up with [the same Slowgirl].
He's such a cocksnot. I don't know, Marybeth's not really,
like, retarded? but I mean, something's definitely wrong.

I mean, she does math at like a second grade level and her mouth is always kind of half-open, you know? It's not Down syndrome, it's like—I don't know what it is. I think when her mom was pregnant with Marybeth she took some drugs to clear up her skin problem or something, and that's what did it?—that's what everyone says. Anyway, so Jessie was like, "We should totally invite Slowgirl. Wouldn't that be hilarious?" And I know it sounds really mean but seriously? Slowgirl has no idea when someone's making fun of her. I mean she's like a golden retriever—I know how awful that sounds, but as long as she's getting attention from someone, she's like, in heaven. *(beat)* Why are you making that face? So when I heard they were gonna invite Slowgirl, I knew how psyched she'd be, so I was like, why not, you know? So Jessie's older brother bought a bunch of vodka and we ended up making Jell-O shots and—none of us knew it or anything but Jell-O's like Slowgirl's favorite food, I mean, she can eat it like 24/7, so we're out in the lawn dancing and everything and we forgot Slowgirl was even at the party. Then someone goes into the kitchen and Slowgirl's in there, wolfing down Jell-O shots, like one after another and we're like, "Marybeth, this isn't just Jell-O. You're only supposed to have two or three." So we hid the rest from her and . . . she seemed like she was fine, I mean, she's a big girl, not like, that fat, but her shoulders are like *(physicalizing it)* and . . . I don't know, she seemed like she was OK. And then I don't really know what happened next 'cause me and Tyler were in Jessie's parents' bedroom the whole time—my parents don't know that part, just so you know. And that's when Marybeth fell out. Tch. My mom left that part out? I'm not surprised, actually. Yeah, Marybeth went up to Jessie's dad's office on the second floor and then she climbed out a window and fell onto the concrete by the pool.

Information on this playwright may be found at:
www.smithandkraus.com.
Click on the AUTHORS tab.

SLOWGIRL
Greg Pierce

Dramatic
Becky, late teens

Becky is talking to her uncle Sterling, who lives in the Costa Rican jungle. Becky has come for a visit, basically to lay low because a girl from her school fell out of a window and is in a coma—and Becky may be responsible.

BECKY: Oh, you guys probly smoke up like twice a day. I would, if I lived here. Whatever, you don't have to tell me. *(long pause)* What's really screwing me over now is, some of it's on tape. Marybeth falling and all that. It's on tape. I had no idea but someone down on the lawn had like an old-school video camera and, whatever, it ended up with the police. I guess they were like, filming goofy stuff like people dancing and dry humping each other and stuff—I don't know, I didn't see it—but I guess then the camera goes up and you see Marybeth way up in the window and she flaps her wings a few times and then she just falls. I mean, it's crazy 'cause the swimming pool's literally touching the side of the house, I mean, Jessie's dad had it built that way so they could see inside the pool from a window in the basement and, I mean, they never ended up doing the window 'cause they were afraid the glass would break and it would flood the house but still, the pool's like right there, I mean, if you or I stepped out of the window, we'd have to like *try* not to land in the deep end. It just—it makes no sense whatsoever. It's like she was trying to hit the concrete. Tanya told me that right before Slowgirl got up on the ledge, you can see me up in the window like, laughing and adjusting her wing but she said you can basically only see my arm and that's so fucked up 'cause I wasn't even there. I was definitely like, helping her attach the wing earlier for like a few seconds but that was at least a half-hour before. So either it's someone else's arm or someone fucked with the tape.

Information on this playwright may be found at:
www.smithandkraus.com.
Click on the AUTHORS tab.

Dramatic

Shafana, twenty-three. Afghani

Safana, a college biology student, is rehearsing a speech, half to her Aunt, half to the audience.

SHAFANA: You get to a point, OK, why don't I be honest, you get to an age and you've absorbed so much and you've observed so much, that you think that you know, basically, what the world has to offer. You've seen it all. Or at least variations of it all. And it's not that you're tired or arrogant or lazy, although they're not the worst things you can be. It's a survival thing. If you're smart and if you've been through a lot, and who hasn't, you can at least congratulate yourself on your ability to vaguely see what might be coming next. To be able to predict situations and not be disorientated. Oh, you don't mind being pleasantly surprised. But you don't like to be caught entirely off guard. It's what separates successful people from other people isn't it? Foresight. And you work at it too, at 'keeping up' and 'keeping in touch' because if you do, you're not going to be fooled. You've sussed out most probabilities so you're ahead of the game. Which is canny. But there always comes a point where you lose it. Where a whole generation lose touch. They start to listen to what looks like the next thing. It sounds like the next thing and it acts like that next thing but it's not the next thing. The truly astonishing thing about what's coming next is that it's nothing like what this generation were like, old or young. It's utterly unfamiliar. If you're a scientist you have to guard against false assumptions. You've all heard the cliché about having to recognize the veil of knowing and surrender to unknowing. But knowing or thinking you know the answers is only one veil. There are others, like physical barriers to seeing. We still don't know half of what is in the deep, deep oceans because they're veiled with darkness. But the creatures are there. Growing, changing, like nothing we've ever seen before. To be discovered. Like the future. Which is not just veiled by time but also by the eyes we're looking at it with. Yes? What if I told you that in the future you might make a choice that today, right now, you would utterly deny. What if I told you that a change is coming, for you, that is so unbelievable that it would make you laugh out loud if I mentioned it.

Information on this playwright may be found at:
www.smithandkraus.com.
Click on the AUTHORS tab.

Dramatic
Sarrinah, forty-three, Afghani

Sarrinah is talking to her niece Shafana, a biology student,
about what Afghanistan was like under the Taliban.

SARRINAH: At the National Museum they used sledge hammers to destroy artworks that were deemed blasphemous. At the Kabul zoo the animals were killed or left to starve. In Mazar-i-Sharif and in Bamiyan they shot dead 8,000 people. Then they forbade the corpses to be buried for six days. This is not a story on the evening news. This is what they did. You do not reason with fanatics. You do not argue with zealots. Their whole work is one rule and one law and one way of being. When we were escaping through Pakistan, the dealers told us that I had to wear a chador, the garment with only one window at the front. We were to get on a bus from Pakistan to India, with me disguised in this chador. It was so hot and there were maybe one hundred people packed onto this bus. We had to crawl over other peoples legs and bodies to get into the bus. I could hardly breathe. We had to sit with our knees pressed up against the bars on the windows and more and more I was struggling for breath. The window at the front of the chador was disappearing, my mouth was covered and I was suffocating on mouthfuls of material. I could not breathe and I thought I was going to die. I thought I was going to be sick. The air was in my throat but wouldn't go down into my lungs, I was suffocating. I was underwater, holding my breath until my lungs involuntarily sucked down wads of cotton and I could not breathe. I pulled the front of the garment up to here. And there was a shout. Get off the bus. You. You there. Get off the bus now. Everyone was looking at us. The soldiers were pointing at us. Get off the bus now. They had guns. They were pointing guns at us and they are not small handguns, these are black Russian guns, AK47's. Get off the bus now. The soldiers had recognized that we were not Pakistani. Because I lifted up the veil? I don't know. Because the chador was whiter than the others on the bus? I don't know. Because of the way I was wearing it, I don't know. They put us in jail. The Pakistani jails have no water. No food. People just go to the toilet anywhere. And now we were going to be sent back to Afghanistan. They drove us to the border, we saw the Afghani flag at the border and that's when the dealers came for us again. They took us back on their ute, we got back on that bus and finally we went through the checkpoint. This took us nine days. With no shower, our clothes were stiff with dirt and the whole time I had to wear this . . . . tent.

Information on this playwright may be found at:
www.smithandkraus.com.
Click on the AUTHORS tab.

Dramatic
Uta, late twenties

Uta Hagen has returned to Ten Chimneys, *the Wisconsin estate of Alfred Lunt and Lynn Fontanne, where a few years previously she rehearsed the Lunts' production of* The Seagull, *in which she played Nina. She has been estranged from the Lunts ever since. Here, she is talking to a man who manages the estate.*

UTA: Do you remember driving me to Milwaukee late one night so I could catch a train? My mother died that night. By the time I got there, the doctors said I couldn't go into her room, that if she saw me she'd realize how serious her condition was—so I never saw her alive again. After the funeral, I went back to New York and we started rehearsals. Everyone was very kind, Mr. Lunt and Miss Fontanne were very kind.
    (beat)
We were doing "The Sea Gull." On Broadway. I'd gotten good notices, and my agent called me to say I had an offer to be in a new show when "The Sea Gull" closed. It was a comedy, for Broadway, the part was perfect for me. All that had to happen was that the Lunts release me from going on the tour. But they said no. "It's the height of unprofessionalism to leave one show for another." I'd signed a contract to go on the road for nine months just like the rest of the cast. So I did.
    (beat)
We were doing "The Sea Gull." We were in Philadelphia. It was a Sunday night, after a four show weekend, very hot. I was in my room at the hotel. I was exhausted, I hadn't slept for days—so I took a pill, just one so I could

sleep through the night. At the hospital the doctor said I'd swallowed a dozen. Miss Fontanne and Mr. Lunt were so concerned they sent me to a psychiatrist. He told them I wasn't in any condition to continue the tour and should be released from my contract. They said no. "The stage is the best medicine." So I stayed.

(beat)

We were doing "The Seagull." Chicago. I was standing in the wings, waiting for my cue. In the last act Nina is supposed to have gone mad. All during rehearsals, I couldn't understand how a simple, happy young girl could suddenly go mad. And then I remembered something Sydney said in this room about his wife. He said she'd never been well, he just hadn't noticed. I realized Nina didn't *suddenly* go mad. She'd *always* been this troubled, erratic, unstable personality, but all the men misread the symptoms of distress as signs of passion and fire. In a flash, I knew how to do the role, start to finish. And then I noticed how quiet it was on stage. I looked and there was Mr. Lunt. He'd just said my entrance cue. If I went on, the audience would never notice. And then I thought how they wouldn't let me go, and I couldn't quit. So I stood there. Mr. Lunt said his line again. I didn't move. Then he said it a third time. And then I went on. The next morning I left the company. They didn't try to stop me this time. They moved on to the next town. They were doing "The Seagull."

Dramatic

Carlotta, mid to late thirties

Carlotta has travelled to Spain along with her editor, Becky, to do some research for a magazine article she is writing about St. Teresa of Avila. She has just returned from Avila, and here she tells her estranged husband Andrés, whom she is finally divorcing after living apart from him for many years, what she saw in Avila, and the effect it had on her.

CARLOTTA: Inside another glass case is her finger, still wearing her emerald ring. Her body never decomposed! Supposedly, a year after she was buried, the nuns kept smelling this bouquet aroma emanating from her tomb inside the wall. So they opened it, and found that the wood of the coffin had rotted, and her clothes were moldy. But her body was intact. So they bathed her, dressed her and presented her to a priest, decided he'd cut one of her hands off, her left hand, and cut for himself a finger to carry around his neck until the day he died. That's the finger inside the display. And years later that same priest again visited Teresa's coffin, and again chopped off some more. Her heart had been pierced by an angel's arrow one day while she prayed at the altar. Now, it's inside a glass jar, with the hole still visible. Teresa wrote about that phenomenon as excruciatingly painful, yet the most pleasurable sensation driving her to moan in rapturous ecstasy. That's all. I think that priest visited Teresa's body one last time, because I hear that pieces of her are dispersed throughout churches in Europe, as relics for veneration. When I was inside the Cathedral, standing next to a huge beam of stone facing a statue of the Virgin Mary and her child . . . I suddenly felt a force of energy travel through me and a strong presence. I turned to my right and there before me stood a little girl in a yellow dress with a familiar face, staring at me. She was me. And seeing again that pretty yellow dress, bare legs, matching socks, shiny white shoes, and pigtails, I felt my heart fill with an overwhelming sense of compassion. Then she walked over to Becky and kissed her on the forehead. A kiss I felt on my lips. We spent that entire day in the Cathedral, but it felt as though only a second had gone by.

Seriocomic
Grete, twenties

Grete is talking to a young man who has met in a bar. He has brought her back to his apartment.

GRETE: If we're gonna fuck we probably should right after these. I'm just saying, it's late, I'm getting sleepy . . . If I had wanted to rest up I would have just gone to bed. I didn't skip my elevator and walk up all those stairs to keep talking about what's his name though. Eeeenough already . . . "everyone here seems to be living in a perpetual reach to attain" or, like, whatever you were saying. You realize that doesn't even make sense. Like, phonetically. Just stop caring so much. Stop caring about shit you don't want to care about. You seem endlessly plagued by things that are out of your control. It just seems silly to me. Caring about the things you have to care about is enough without adding all this extraneous bullshit. You're not as important as you think you are. They probably haven't given any of that half as much thought as you have. You might find it freeing to realize how little you matter. Don't ask me, just take me and, you're right we think everything is what it isn't, I thought for sure there's a guy who will fuck me not just be a complete pussy, not just go on and on but a guy that will just grab me. I just wanted a fun time. Not a philosophy class.

Information on this playwright may be found at:
www.smithandkraus.com.
Click on the AUTHORS tab.

THE FUTURE IS NOT WHAT IT WAS
Michael Rabe

Dramatic
Laura, twenties

Laura is talking to a rather callow young man who lives in her apartment building.

LAURA: When I was little, my mom was going on a boat, a dinner party on a boat. And she invited me. But I didn't want to go. I did. But I said I didn't. And I was down half way down the driveway under this pine tree. And I figured she'd come double check before she left. And then I'd say yes and go. And I hear her car coming down the driveway and know she'll slow down so I'm coming out from under the tree right as her car passes. Certain that she'll see me and stop. I'm right there. But she keeps going. And I start running as fast as I can. Screaming and screaming because I really want to go. And then I trip and I fall and cut my chin. Right here, you see? But she just kept driving. And I could never tell her about how I'd been chasing the car. And I never got to go to that dinner party on a boat. And I've always wanted to
    (beat)
and every time I see this scar it reminds me of that. Of that place I'll never be able to get to again. Or never got to, I guess.

Information on this playwright may be found at:
www.smithandkraus.com.
Click on the AUTHORS tab.

Dramatic
Celia, mid-thirties

CELIA is speaking to her younger sister, Amy. Amy has just come home to tell Celia that she's written a book about their mother, a troubled alcoholic who died in a car accident years earlier. Celia was her mother's de facto caretaker in her later years while Amy was living in the city pursuing her artistic dreams. She is vehemently against Amy publishing the book, as she feels Amy cannot tell this story, having not been there in her mother's final days, nor on her final night.

CELIA: You want to know why mom drove herself home that night? I was taking a drawing class. I didn't tell anyone. I just had the crazy thought that maybe I could go back to school-focus more on my art. That night was bad—I almost didn't go—I was fucking dreading class. We were working on figure drawing with charcoal, and I was terrible at it. It was all big hands and tiny heads. My people looked like victims of that drug pregnant women were taking back in the seventies. Awful. But I had this incredible teacher—Sam—I never had a teacher who told us to call him by his first name before. And Sam kept telling me it would happen if I kept working. And that I had a gift even if I couldn't see it yet. So that night I made myself go. I picked up a piece of charcoal and I went to work on my tiny heads. And I started to cry a little bit, if you can believe it. Just to myself. Sam saw I was having a meltdown and he came over. He took the charcoal out of my hand and handed me a pallet with three blobs of red, yellow, and blue paint. He told me to take a good look at the model, his thigh muscles, the way his stomach moved. And then he turned my easel around so my back was to the model I was supposed to be drawing. I was like, 'what the hell am I supposed to do now?' And he said, 'don't look back. Just paint.' I started with one red splotch. Then I did another. Then it just took over. It was like I was above myself looking down at my hands moving across the page in these big stripes of color. I painted the entire easel, the mat the paper was clipped to. I would have moved to the walls if Sam hadn't stopped me. He looked at what I had done and he said, "Well there you are. I was wondering when we'd find you."

(CELIA is a little bit choked up though she'd never admit it.)

When I looked around, everyone was starting to pack up. Class was over. But I wasn't finished. I was vibrating, I was hovering above the floor. Sam said, 'Stay. If you want. The door will lock behind you.' So I stayed.

(beat)

When I got to the bar, her usual stool was empty. I think you know the rest. A fucking drawing class.

(beat)

I've rewritten a million versions in my head. What if I hadn't stayed. What if I showed up? What if mom made it home? What if you stayed here? What if I left? What if, what if.

Information on this playwright may be found at:
www.smithandkraus.com.
Click on the AUTHORS tab.

Seriocomic
Lia, seventeen Asian (Hmong) American

Lia, in the gym during a volleyball game, has this stream-of-consciousness monologue.

LIA: On the court, warming up, a pep talk. I talk to myself. I know. It's a habit you pick up when you play like we do. Sharp. Focused. "Bitch's talking to herself," I hear from the other side of the net, a girl. A monster. A blonde. "Fucking Korean girl's talking to herself." Fucking Korean? Fucking Korea's far away. And so's everything else. The house. The land. Everything except here. Everything except this. That. Them. So this fucking Korean says nothing. She just swallows her words, her thoughts, her Gatorade. 'Cause I got a game to set up for. I'm the heart of the team. The setter. I get us going, I get us pumped. I tag in, I tag out I weave between the players, the poles, past the out lines and back to my seat on the bench, as the game moves along. Point after point, I break. I batter. I mow them down. But still it's a close match. A neck and neck. With every bump. Set. Spike. Got it! Call it! Chance! Tag in. Tag out. Bump up. Punch out, Lia. Move, Xiong. The face of my teammate stares down at me, waiting to take my place. But I don't. I can't. All I want is another minute. Moment. Another fifteen . . . fourteen . . . thirteen seconds until—I shrug her off and I rotate into view. Of the blonde. The giant. The Scandinavian monster. "Das Goliath." And even if I'm too far grounded to see the whites of her eyes, she's mine. 'Cause they don't know, but I can fly. Way over the net, over the heads and shoulders of the opposing team. I leap into the air—and see a girl. Just like me, same face, same wondering expression. I see her and—OW! JEEZ.

(LIA clutches her face. She's been hit)
The ball. The floor. The blood streams from my nose, down my shirt, onto the court as the final buzzer goes off. I look around—And nothing.

TIME IN KAFKA
Len Jenkin

Dramatic
Sturdza, "a woman of a certain age"

*Principessa Sturdza, a woman of a certain age, speaking
to a younger woman about the mysteries of love.*

STURDZA: One evening many years ago, I went to the opera
in Venice. I was with an Italian duke, handsome as a god,
and just as wealthy. As the audience gathered in front of
La Fenice, an old Chinese gentleman appeared, pulling
a bamboo cage on wheels. In the cage was a black bear.
The old man took a long spoon and a jar of honey from
under his robe and fed the bear, sliding the dripping
spoon between the bars into the bear's mouth. Then he
opened the cage door. The bear shuffled out and stood
up on its hind legs. It wore a red cap. The man talked to
it gently in Mandarin, then blew on a tiny flute. The bear
swayed in place, then began a heavy-footed shuffle, side
to side. The doors of La Fenice opened, we threw a few
coins, and went inside. I saw them again as I was leaving
Venice. The duke had accused me of stealing an emerald
necklace of his mother's, and had called the police. I was
embarking at twilight. The bear in its cage was being
hoisted by a dockside crane aboard my ship, a freighter
sailing for Morocco and Cadiz. The Chinese gentleman
watched from the dock. Suddenly the cable snapped, and
the caged bear plunged down into the black water. The
old man howled in agony. The cage sank quickly. The
red sun followed it slowly into the Venetian lagoon, and
the first stars appeared in the darkening sky. The Chinese
gentleman boarded the ship. We sailed off into the night
and the Adriatic. I saw him at the rail near midnight. He
took his long spoon out from under his robe, dipped it

in the jar of honey, and tossed it into the sea. Make of it what you will, cherie. It's true. The bear is at the bottom of the Venetian lagoon. Fish swim by his eyes.

Seriocomic
Woman, mid-forties

*A middle-aged woman tells a teenaged boy waiting for the
bus that she is his mother. (It isn't true)*

WOMAN: Well, ok . . . what if that night, after you were
delivered and sent home with your Dad, ok what if
I suddenly came to? What if they had given me this
powerful sedative while I was giving birth, lexi-
something, and I flat lined. But Dr. Stevenson, my
ob/gyn, he used those paddle things and he brought
me back to life. And what if when I came to I had
amnesia—from the drugs and the paddles and shock.
And what if Dr. Stevenson had always been a little in
love with me, since Schenectady even, and when he
discovered I had amnesia and couldn't remember you
or your Dad, he told me that he was my husband. That
a new job had opened up in Long Island and we would
have to be moving as soon as I was feeling better from
my appendectomy. So we moved, and had a family,
a family of tennis players. But it wasn't my fault, or
anyone's really. And then the other day, in Long Island,
we were playing doubles, and your half sister, Helen,
she hit a lob, and I went back and your half brother,
Troy, he came forward, and Troy's so uber competitive,
he jump slammed his return, and whacked me in the
head with his racket. I got concussed, but it shook free
this memory, this memory of a little boy, with a little
blue hat, who smelt like me and paradise combined,
a baby named Robert who I loved more than my new
children and who I had to find at all costs, who I had
to put my arm around

(she does this)
who I had to tell: Your mother is here. She loves you. She
never meant to leave you. And now she's here.

Information on this playwright may be found at:
www.smithandkraus.com.
Click on the AUTHORS tab.

Comic
Cassandra, could be any age.

Cassandra is a housekeeper at a house in Bucks County owned by Masha, a famous movie star, who has arrived for a visit with her latest boyfriend, a handsome hunk named Spike who is half her age. Spike has met a cute girl named Nina who lives nearby who's a big fan of Masha. Cassandra is given to premonitions of doom. This is one of them.

CASSANDRA: Lunch will be a little delayed. I dropped the omelets on the floor. I'm going to have to start over.
> *(sees NINA, points at her)*

What did I say? BEWARE OF NINA! Nina, Hootie Pie, mushrooms, wind, tornados—beware of them all!
> *(feels drawn to make a bit of a speech)*

Oh mystery and misery, descends upon me like a thunder cloud,
Pregnant with rain and Jupitor's arrows.
The terrible burden of true prophecy, of my unwanted but unstoppable prelude.
Look out, look out—all around us are lions and tigers and bears.
Oh my the omelette is a failure, I crush it beneath my foot.

The libation bearers bring guts and entrails
And parents' children chopped up and served in a shepherd's pie.
Something tastes wrong with it—little wonder!
Next time you won't go killing Agamemnon, will you?
He's already dead. My car needs to be inspected,

How can I keep all these facts in my head when I see
calamity and colossus
Lumbering up the walkway?
Oh wretches, oh misery, oh magical mystery tour.
Beware the future. I know you will not abide me,
You ignore because I am not tall.
But I am right! I see disaster ahead for all of you!
Lunch in about 20 minutes!

Information on this playwright may be found at:
www.smithandkraus.com.
Click on the AUTHORS tab.

VENUS IN FUR
David Ives

Dramatic
Vanda, twenties

Vanda, an actress, is auditioning for Thomas, who has written and is directing a play based on a notorious, sado-masochistic 19th century novel. Her audition has become far more than just an audition by this point, as she and Thomas basically become the characters in the novel, and as we begin to wonder if, perhaps, Wanda is something far more than just an actress.

VANDA: How does your Significant Other feel about this play? She's probably worried you've got this whole kinky side and she doesn't want you to put this play on because people will think this might be you. Or her. But let me guess about Stacy. She's a little younger than you. Good family. Grew up in one of those nice old stone houses. Maybe Connecticut. Southwestern Massachusetts, near the Connecticut border. Twenty minutes from Litchfield. Am I close? She's tall. Maybe a little bossy, in a nice way. Lots of hair, long legs, big brain. Probably went to Stanford. Am I close? Maybe even a Ph.D. Well? She's got a dog. Let's see. Maybe a Weimaraner. That you like okay but could secretly do without, named something like . . . something traditional, something Old Testament and manly. Like . . . Seth. Ezra. I bet she's the breadwin-ner, too. I mean, a room with a pipe in the middle of it? Not exactly the big bucks on Broadway. She probably came with money, but while she finishes up her thesis she's working some nice investment job. Or day-trading and making a fortune. Am I right? I'm right. But hey, you're an artist. She loves that about you. And she just knows you're going to be a great big success someday. Plus she appreciates you for your sensitivity. Maybe you're the first guy she met who's got any. She reads a lot. Same books you do. Likes the opera and the ballet and shit. Like you. At night you talk about what's going on in French philosophy and what's new in the New York Review of Books, then you have some nice quiet sex. And nice quiet sex is fine. Though there's this rumbling at the back of your head. This voice that wants something else. I don't know what that is, but . . . *Rumble, rumble, rumble.* Anyway, hey, you're happy. You *like* her. You really, really like her and you two are going to have a nice life talking about French philosophy and what's in the New York Review of Books and maybe have a couple of kids who can do that when they grow up. And then you'll die.

Information on this playwright may be found at:
www.smithandkraus.com.
Click on the AUTHORS tab.

WALTER CRONKITE IS DEAD
Joe Calarco

Comic
Patty, fifties

*A fierce storm has shut down all the airports on the eastern
seaboard. Patty, a chatty southerner, strikes up a conversation with a woman in the waiting area while they wait for
word about whether or not their flights are cancelled.*

PATTY: Breathe. That's what *I* gotta do. All this terrible,
terrible weather. Can you imagine all the missed connections, the ruined vacations? These storms just add up to
hundreds of teeny, tiny, unexpected, little heartbreaks.
But me? I have Jackie Joy in my corner. The best con-
cierge in all of London if my opinion counts for anything.
Do you know what she did?
   (not waiting for a response)
She got our *Lion King* tickets switched. Why I said to
her, "Jackie dear, we don't know when we're gonna be
getting outta here. There are storms a-raging." "Jackie,"
I said, "Now our flight might just be leaving here on
time." That's what I told her. "But then again it might
not. We might not leave at all today. There is no way to
tell at this time, and I am not going to miss my chance to
see the greatest theatrical event of the century." And the
changes she's had to make. My daughter and I've been
doing these trips abroad for years, ever since she was a
little thing, saving every single penny I can to do it. I'll
do without the other fifty weeks of the year as long as I
can have these two. Had to take on a second job this year
to afford it, but no mind, it's always been very important
to me, the one luxury I allow myself 'cause I think it's
important for her to see, but—Well this year she changed
her mind. Threw everything up into a tizzy. Jackie's

had to scramble to get everything changed from two a' this and two a' that to just one for little old me. But I'm glad. I am. She was making a fuss about all the arrangements anyhow. That's why I'm stuck here. She wanted to go to New York first. If we had just gone straight on to London out of BWI we'd have probably just missed these storms. We' be over the Atlantic by now. But no . . . "Mama why don't we stop in New York first and see it there?" Have you ever? It's London. I don't care what they say about the Broadway. London is where it all started—you know, the theater and all. And I said to her. "Well get ready to see it twice 'cause I'm getting us tickets to see it in London too and I'll prove it to you. They're just better over there." The actors. It's a fact. And do you know what she said to me?

(PATTY dives into her purse rummaging around for something.)

Wait, wait, wait… I wrote it down. I started to keep track of some of the sayings she throws my way. I had to have some proof, something to point to and say, "See, see what I've had to put up with."

(She pulls out a pocket size notepad)

Aha! Wait til you hear this. "Yes Mother—" She calls me Mother when she really wants to get at me. "Yes Mother, I'm sure the British hyenas will be much more accomplished than the Broadway hyenas." Have you ever? That mouth of hers. I don't know where that came from. I always thought she loved the theatre. Do you know what she wanted instead? She wanted to see a *play*, saying British film actors go back to the stage all the time. "We could see a movie star in a play Mama. Think of that," and do you wanna know who she mentioned? Maggie Smith. Well, I shot down that idea lickity split let me tell you. I don't like that one. Walking around in all her pictures like she's better than everyone, with her accent and her way of talking and just the way she *looks* at people. I bet they have to close down those movie sets for her every day, so she can have her tea—and little biscuits—just so she can feel better than the rest of us, and I always feel just a little bit dumber sitting there staring up at her. And her eyes bug out. She scares me.

Information on this playwright may be found at:
www.smithandkraus.com.
Click on the AUTHORS tab.

Lawrence Harbison

Comic
Patty, fifties

A fierce storm has shut down all the airports on the eastern seaboard. Patty, a chatty southerner, has struck up a conversation with a woman in the waiting area while they wait for word about whether or not their flights are cancelled.

PATTY: I remember wanting to go see *The Exorcist* when it first came out, and well my sister said to me, "Patty, don't do it. Don't go. It is the scariest movie I ever did see." So of course I grabbed my husband Marty and we went that very same night. And let me tell you, it was more than being scared. I was *disturbed* by that. The whole country was *disturbed*. Pastors preached on it. News articles. Magazine covers. It shook the country. All of us were looking for the Devil around every two and one half corners. And I knew. I knew from the very beginning with all that sand blowing around and that Arab man with one eye and that scary idol, statue thing. I knew it was not gonna end up right.
  (She takes a nail file out and works on her nails.)
It was The *Ex-or-cist*. It wasn't the bogeyman in the closet or "Boo!" jumping out from around the corner or any of those—What did they call 'em?—slasher movies that started cropping up. That Jamie Lee Curtis. I got so mad at her. "Look behind you girl! He's right there." We all knew he wasn't gonna be dead. But there she sat all crying and all. "Get out of the house Jamie Lee! He's a psychotic killer and he's still in the house dead or no. Leave!" Do you think if her mama had known for one second that Anthony Perkins had stuffed his mother and

then kept her body up in that bedroom that she would've stuck around and taken a shower? Nuh, uh, uh.

(She imitates the Psycho shower stabbing noises.)
I'm telling you, she'd have been smarter. She'd have gotten herself out of there. So I don't know what her little Jamie Lee was thinking all curled up weeping and wailing. That's just stupid. All those stupid movies with those stupid teenagers doing stupid things. But The *Exorcist.* This was—this was evil. Evil creeping into that lovely Ellyn Burstyn's rented house right here in Georgetown. Evil. In *Georgetown.* Well, I'm sorry but I was like, "If it could happen in Georgetown, it certainly could happen in Tennessee." And that poor little Linda Blair. How do you survive something like that? I know it was just a movie, and pretending is fine and all—but don't start pretending with the Devil. Don't start pretending with real life 'cause as sure as Linda Blair had no career to speak of after that movie, you will pay for that.

Information on this playwright may be found at:
www.smithandkraus.com.
Click on the AUTHORS tab.

Seriocomic
Erin, early thirties

Erin reprimands her husband, a playwright, for overreaching in his choice of professions.

ERIN: George, you're a big boy. For whatever reason, the choice to write whatever the hell you're writing was obviously yours. Frankly I have no sympathy for writers who find themselves in these kinds of jams, where they lose focus of what they started out to do and then go into a panic mode like you're doing now. Life is too short for someone as exquisitely uncomplicated as myself to put up with this chaotic and desperate behavior and I don't know how much longer I can or will. It's selfish and it's unfair. I don't want to upset you any more than you are but it's very possible playwriting isn't for you. Your talent may not be as lofty as your ambition and once again you're over reaching. Maybe it's time to think about other areas that are not as demanding as the theatre, like television for instance. That could solve everything. The expectations in that field are far less and the pay checks are far more. It's something to really consider. Anyway, I'm off to the gym. With any luck, when I get back, you'll have pulled yourself together and given what I just said some serious thought. Goodbye for now, George. I wish I could be more encouraging than honest. It's sometimes very confusing which is the more valued quality. Sometimes I really worry about you, even if it seems I don't.

Information on this playwright may be found at:
www.smithandkraus.com.
Click on the AUTHORS tab.

Comic
Karen, thirties to forties

Karen is talking to her dog. It's morning. She hasn't been to work all week.

KAREN: I see you looking at me. I know what you're thinking. You're thinking I should get dressed and go to work. "Get going," your eyes say. But I am moving. You might not see it, but I'm moving. It's slow sure, but I'm faster than erosion. Faster than continental drift. But wait a minute. Let me rest. What's the hurry? Live in the moment here with me. I'm here right now and I aim to stay here for another few minutes, an hour, a day. Everything will go on without me. I didn't go to work yesterday or the day before and yet the world continues to revolve. New York does not need me. People go about their lives. No one calls to ask where I am. It's like I don't exist at all. But I do exist don't I? Your mouth says yes but your eyes say no. Please stop judging me. I don't need to go to work, not today. It won't affect the food in your dish. You'll get fed. And you won't be lonely. Please don't say anything. I know you disapprove and I hear you but it's really not what I want right now and I know you subscribe to a sort of tough love viewpoint, but sometimes that's not very helpful and furthermore, not appreciated. Don't look at me like that. I do appreciate you, just not the hard line you try to draw sometimes. The world is not black and white. And colors can be confusing, so let me sit and rest and figure out a few things, okay? It'll be fun. I can stay here all day with you. We can watch bad romantic comedies and you can jump up on the bed and curl up

with me and we can eat crackers if we want. I won't
kick you out. And tomorrow?

    (beat)

Who knows? Let's just think of today. Everything is so
uncertain these days.

Information on this playwright may be found at:
www.smithandkraus.com.
Click on the AUTHORS tab.

Comic

Adelaide, African American, sixties (although in class or for auditions actress could be any age)

Adelaide is talking to her son Gil, still a struggling actor at age forty.

ADELAIDE: I almost died yesterday. A curse! I simply asked her to take off her shoes when she came in the door. You know I don't like people tracking their lives in my house. She looked at me kind of funny. Then I made the mistake of asking her to use a coaster for her pineapple spritzer and she looked at me kinda sideways! And when she got up to use the bathroom, I simply told her I laid out hand towels, chile, you woulda thought I told her that Ike Turner was in there waiting for her! And then, during our ladies lunch she proceeded to contradict everything I said. If I said the sky was blue—she said that she wasn't so sure. For the life of me, I don't know why Lavinia would bring someone like that to my elegant home. Well, I found out when Shavon, Sherelle or whatever her name was, was in the bathroom that Lavinia was her host. This woman was at least sixty and from Haiti. Mmm hmm, she was staying with Lavinia for free in exchange for light housekeeping duties. Now, Ms. Lavinia may be a big-ole thick woman who laughs like a man who's got some unfortunate cankles, but she is SMART! Chevron just kept staring at me in a funny way and muttering something under her breath. It was witchcraft or something! Ooohh girl, you should have seen her. She was just as evil as sin. She was wearing this tight brown dress cutting off all her circulation and those men's work boots? Timberlands. What sixty-something year old woman wears Timberlands? And I am GIVING her sixty-something because she looked as old as Methuselah! She was wearing Timberlands and I was suspect! She had the thinnest hair I've ever seen on a grown woman. Her hair was real thin and was pulled to the back in a couple of plats. I guess she was fussing with it in the bathroom cause when she came out it was everywhere. Honey, it look like she had a head full of baby hair! She was evil. You know women who can't grow no hair are evil. I am sure she took one look at my thick Indian hair and reached for her spells and potions. The moment she and Ms. Lavinia left I started getting sick. I told you she was Haitian, didn't I? SHE PUT A CURSE ON ME! My face got all swole up, I started throwing up and I had a fever. I felt sick as a dog and my hair itched.

(pause)

If the UPS man didn't show up with my Limited Edition Genuine Porcelain Cinderella Doll from the QVC, I would be speaking to you from beyond the grave right now.

Comic

Aunt Glo, African American, fifties to sixties (although for class or auditions, actress could be any age)

Aunt Glo's sister has died. She has come to the funeral home to see about the arrangements. She is speaking to Terry, the son of the owner, who works there.

AUNT GLO: The community is supposed to come together: To plan! To support! To grieve! Don't nobody need anybody anymore? Now everybody is grieving on their own. I think the "internets" are the problem. Can I please have a glass of water?

(TERRY goes to get the water)

First there was dial up but then apparently that was too slow! Everybody telling me I gotta get that DSL cable. Why? I got HBO and Showtime! But they said I would be able to surf and get online and chat and things like that.

(TERRY returns with the water)

MICROWAVE OVENS! Thank you. Good looks run in the family. You look just like all the other Terrys! Good looks get the grieving widows to spend all of they insurance money on the funeral services hunh? Mmm hmmm. Anyway. Everybody just stays online and stays to themselves. No real relationships. The "internets" are keeping families apart. Adelaide, my sister, God rest her soul, even had one of them SPACEBOOK accounts set up by Gil so that she could keep up with him. If I gotta find out what going on with you on a page over the "internets"—there is a problem. What, nobody know how to pick up a phone anymore??? No, because there is texting and "twitching" going on. You know, Gil told me that, that is the way he lets folks know what is happening moment to moment. No one needs to know what is going on with you moment to moment unless they are THERE! You ain't there then somebody will TELL you about it. Go over their house and tell 'em about it. Have a piece of pie and talk. Or not talk just be together. That is called communication! I am so sorry do you have a dead body to burn or anything right now.

Comic

Aunt Glo, African American, fifties to sixties (although for class or auditions, actress could be any age)

Aunt Glo's sister Adelaide has died. Gil, her nephew, has cremated Adelaide and has taken her urn to Disney World to scatter the ashes.

AUNT GLO: YOU HAVE LOST YOUR MIND! You can't have no funeral services in DISNEY WORLD! I don't know what has been filling your head, excuse my French, LIVING LA VIDA LOCA, but when a person dies, Praise Jesus, there are supposed to be funeral services. A church, a choir, a program, flowers, a casket, help me father, A CASKET! NOT AN URN! What kind of word is that anyway? URNNNNN!!! A wreathe of flowers on the door! You need a wreathe of flowers on the door!!! And a HURST! A HURST!!! Limos for the family with big orange stickers that said funeral on 'em! So other cars know that they shouldn't break the line of cars during the processional. THE PROCESSIONAL!!! What is wrong with you boy? People need a processional! People need to wear black and veils! And WEEP!!! You gotta let people come and weep! FALL OUT and LAY over the casket weep! If they don't weep there, then they could do it at the CEMETERY, where they toss FLOWERS on the CASKET. THE CASKET, not the URN! You don't toss flowers on an URN! Toss flowers on the CASKET AND REACH THEIR GRIEF STRICKEN ARTHRITIC FINGERS TO THE BOWELS OF THE EARTH AS THEIR LOVED ONE IS TAKEN ON AN ELEVATOR TO THEIR FINAL RESTING PLACE SIX FEET UNDER. YOU CAN'T HAVE A FUNERAL SERVICE IN ORLANDO, FLORIDA!!!! YOU CAN'T WEAR BLACK IN FLORIDA!!!

YOU FOR ME FOR YOU
Mia Chung

Comic
Tiffany, late thirties

Tiffany tells her friend Junhee about her date last night.

TIFFANY: When I did graveyard, I thought that was why I couldn't meet anyone. But even with eHarmony, PlentyofFish, match.com and okCupid, I still can't find Mr. Right, the light of my life, Prince Charming, my soul mate. I went on a date last night . . . Disaster. Date from hell. Heinous snafu fiasco. A hot mess. He was late, spilled wine, called me Gina twice, didn't laugh at my jokes, hasn't returned my voicemail or email or friend request or text. I'm really not choosy. All I want is someone nice. Who's honest and funny, works out at least four days a week. Someone who doesn't pinch pennies. Can make conversation. Has beautiful eyes or feet. Likes dogs not cats. Who's handy or knows his way around a kitchen. Reads books. Isn't an only child. World traveler. Graduated from NYU—equivalent or better. Who likes me. I'm learning to stay positive, ask questions, step back and let go. I was feeling blocked, cluttered. So I got a book on simple living, did a cleanse, stripped down my closet And then I discovered all the shoes I had were crap. I'm on my feet all day. And in this city, you need good shoes. They have to be sensible and stylish and feel good and last a long time and go with every outfit, work or play. I definitely need new shoes. Everyone in this city has this problem. And what do we do with all the crappy expensive shoes?! So stupid. So wasteful. So not me. Not anymore. You wonder how it all fit in your closet, your budget, your life? Am I right?

YOUR BOYFRIEND MAY BE IMAGINARY
Larry Kunofsky

Comic
Paula Paul, late twenties or thirties

Paula Paul is presiding over a Divorce Party in her apartment with her soon-to-be-ex-husband, Paul Paul, who at this moment, cannot be found. The mood is festive, but perhaps there is something a little desperate about this festiveness, and perhaps Paul Paul and their guests are trying to hide other, deeper emotions behind the festivities. She is addressing the guests at the Divorce Party, as well as us, the audience.

PAULA PAUL: Look at me! Here comes the ex-bride! Wheeeh! Look at me, wow, dressed in white. Maybe this is not so appropriate now, but then again it wasn't so appropriate then. Hah! Wow, I fit into this dress better than I did when I First Wore It. What did I know about carbs back then. What did I know about lots of things back then. Hah! Anyway, thanks all so much for coming to our Divorce Party and thank you so much for the support over the years and the repetitive and never-ending encouragement you all offered in attempts to get us divorced over the years. Well we're finally doing it! Whoo-hooh! So are we all here? Wait a minute, Where's the Man-of-Honor?! Where's HunkyDave? Hah, I'm kidding, hah. Where's my not-for-very-much-longer husband? Has anyone seen Paul Paul? Oh that man! If I weren't done with him already . . . I'm kidding! I'm kidding, of course. It's all amicable as you all know. Oh well. Carry on and talk among yourselves until he comes back. Then we'll have the ceremony. Thanks everybody. Whoo!

Information on this playwright may be found at:
www.smithandkraus.com.
Click on the AUTHORS tab.

Dramatic
Denise, late twenties or thirties

Denise is having a very late-night phone conversation with her friend Marci, after Marci has spent the whole day and evening looking in vain for her boyfriend. Throughout Marci's quest, Denise has offered to help, but Marci was on her own journey and was unable or unwilling to accept Denise's assistance, or even her friendship. But now, before they fall asleep, Denise explains to Marci how they have both lost someone, and that they are bonded together through their loss.

DENISE: Marci I lost someone too. A while ago like a year ago way before you went through what you've gone through but still what I went through always made me think of you even before this happened. Like when I miss the one I lost I think of you and miss you too not that I lost you but I miss you. And I think even before Phillip you were dealing with Missing Things. I mean this Phillip must have sensed that about you, that that was what you were about, the Missing Things. I guess he figured the best way to be gone from you was just to be gone. To absent himself. Because that's you, Marci, that's just what you're about it's not a judgment it just is. So tonight when you told me you were missing someone actual and specific in particular it became clear why I stayed away from you for so long because I missed you without having you and I was afraid that feeling love for you wasn't fair because I seemed to be mainly loving that thing about you, that Missing Things thing, and I felt bad about that for a long time but then I realized that that Missing Things thing was a really, really big part of who you are and who I am and who we are and that's a good thing so I'm sorry if you find these feelings unsettling because of its terminology but it's a good thing.

Information on this playwright may be found at:
www.smithandkraus.com.
Click on the AUTHORS tab.

Seriocomic
Denise, late twenties or thirties,

Denise has spent a long night worrying about Marci, her friend, who has been out all night searching for her lost boyfriend. After Marci has realized that she will never see her boyfriend again, she goes home, to bed. Denise has called Marci to explain that she, too, has lost someone that she loved. Denise tells Marci the story of the woman she met only once but has loved ever since.

DENISE: So I was sitting at the bar for a long, long time not saying anything to anyone and not even feeling self-conscious about it which was great since it was so rare for me so I was feeling a kind of bliss it was blissful I was blessed. I was blessed. With bliss. But not drunk. That bliss can never be repeated that's what made it so special the one-time-thing-ed-ness of it for me and how everyone there could see that I had this one-time-thing glow about me so I continued unmolested because people didn't bother me with small talk out of respect of my bliss, my glow. So this woman sits down on the stool next to mine and she's got the same exact glow as mine, that blissyglow, and we turn to face each other and we recognize each other's blissyglow and our glows are only enhanced and intensified by our happiness on behalf of the other for possessing this glow, it's not a self-satisfied thing, like oh, I'm glad you've got that glow because that validates my glow, that's *wack*; no, it was a warm, sincere joy. And that gave us license to speak but we didn't speak. We kissed. And it was beautiful. And it was wonderful. And it wasn't sexual all that much but it was way sexy. And such sharp and bright and shimmering happiness kind of like married us together. And our kiss was long and sweet it was like dew on the grass first thing in the morning. It was the drop of a taste from the honeysuckle. It was those blown-away particles from the pussy willow. It was love. Like never before. I've lived the greatest moment of my life and the rest of my life will only be sweeter for it and for knowing that this is so. So we get up to leave. We walk out into the night and the light from a streetlamp illuminates her from behind. Because she was walking in front of me. And the light on her back shows me that she's got this tattoo, this enormous tattoo, it takes up the whole of her back. She he had this mythological creature on her back. This giant red and black and purple winged flaming *being* tattooed on her back with Sanskrit writing kind of like framing it. It was like the ceiling of the Sistine Chapel or something only instead of being on the ceiling of some boring-ass church, it's on the back of this luscious young ridonculously yummy one. I hope that if I ever do go to the Sistine Chapel, I won't be, like, Wow, that's a nice ceiling, because why would you say that unless you're like some doucheclown who always has to be talking and ruining moments for other people and for oneself. So I was so afraid to remark on this masterpiece of a work of art emblazoned behind this masterpiece of a ridonculously yummy one because so far I haven't acted like a dork at all in this story but that may be mostly because I hadn't really said anything at all up to this point. I mean, what, "nice tattoo?" I mean like, way to say what everybody probably says to her every five minutes. But I couldn't not. I mean, sure, as we've already established, saying something about the Sistine Chapel *at* the Sistine Chapel is superfluous at best, but not saying anything about the tattoo on her back would be like going to someone's apartment and realizing that they have the Sistine Chapel on their ceiling and not say anything. So somehow I muster up enough non-dorkitude to say something that actually wasn't stupid. I

Lawrence Harbison

197

said, "What a spiritual work of art your back is," which I know actually does sound stupid although we did both kind of laugh at what I said even at the time but it was at least contextually prescient. So she tells me about it, she says, "I had it done in one sitting, right after I lost my father. It's in honor of him. The Sanskrit passage and the nature of this particular mythological beast speak to me of him." And I was like, Damn. And she told me how painful it was and how the needles, because it was more than one guy with one needle doing her back, it was like a whole staff of artisans, and how it reminded her of the surgeons working on her father to no avail, and yet this was to some avail, to remind her of that very patient, her father, who was being honored by her back, and I said, it was worth it, which is presumptuous of me, I admit, but I said, now you yourself are In Memory of him. That made us both sad for a while but not in a way that ruined anything. So then we realized we couldn't just stand under a streetlight all night and she said, "I can't take you home with me. It'd be like a hook-up. It'd be cheap. And you're worth more than that." And I agreed. And she said, "I love you which I can't believe since we just met even though it's true but since it is true I might as well say it." And I said "I feel totally exactly completely utterly absolutely one hundred percent unbelievably but ultimately unwaveringly the same way." That's word for word what I said. So we decided to go our separate ways. We probably should have exchanged contact information. Maybe that was intentional on her part but on my part it was more about not dealing with the practical and dealing instead with the, y'know, the wonderful. And so we both left but both in our own direction, which was each the opposite of the other's and neither of us ever looked back and so I just kept on walking and I walked all the way home even though you know how far that is but I didn't even have my Defensive Walking Eye out, I just kind of walked like normal and luckily no one bothered me although in my memory it's almost as if no one else was on the street at all which is unlikely but it really feels that way even now and it was only until I got home that I realized I'd never see her again.

Information on this playwright may be found at:
www.smithandkraus.com.
Click on the AUTHORS tab.

Lawrence Harbison

Rights & Permissions

The entire text of a play may be procured from the performance rights holder

AEROSOL DREAMS © 2013 by Nicole Pandolfo. Reprinted by permission of Nicole Pandolfo. For performance rights, contact Nicole Pandolfo (nicole.e.pandolfo@gmail.com).

ALL-AMERICAN © 2012 by Julia Brownell. Reprinted by permission of Chris Till, Creative Artists Agency. For performance rights, contact Dramatists Play Service, 440 Park Ave. S., New York, NY 10016 (www.dramatists.com) (212-683-8960).

AMERICAN STORM by Integrity out of Molly Brown © 2012 by Carter W. Lewis. Reprinted by permission of Susan Gurman, Susan Gurman Agency. For performance rights, contact Susan Gurman (susan@gurmanagency.com).

AMERICA'S BRIGHTEST STAR © 2012 by Alex Goldberg. Reprinted by permission of Alex Goldberg. For performance rights, contact Alex Goldberg (alexstephengoldberg@gmail.com).

THE ANARCHIST © 2012 by David Mamet. Reprinted by permission of Zach Chotzen-Freund, Theatre Communications Group. The entire text of the play has been published by Theatre Communications Group (TCG Books). For performance rights, contact Ron Gwiazda, Abrams Artists Agency (ron.gwiazda@abramsartny.com).

rights, contact Scott Chaloff (schaloff@wmeentertainment.com).

CONEY © 2012 by David Johnston. Reprinted by permission of David Johnston. For performance rights, contact David Johnston (johnstondavidh@gmail.com).

CONSTRUCTION OF THE HUMAN HEART © 2012 by Ross Mueller. Reprinted by permission of Beth Blickers, Abrams Artists Agency. For performance rights, contact Beth Blickers (beth.blickers@abramsartny.com).

DARK RADIO © 2010 by Colin Mckenna. Reprinted by permission of Antje Oegel, AO International. For performance rights, contact Antje Oegel (aoegel@aoegelinternational.com).

DEAD ACCOUNTS © 2012 by Theresa Rebeck. Reprinted by permission of Theresa Rebeck. For performance rights, contact Samuel French, Inc., (212-206-8990, www.samuelfrench.com).

DETROIT © 2011 by Lisa D'Amour. Reprinted by permission of Farrar, Straus & Giroux LLC. For performance rights, contact Dramatists Play Service, 440 Park Ave. S., New York, NY 10016 (www.dramatists.com) (212-683-8960).

THE ELECTRIC BABY © 2012 by Stefanie Zadravec. Reprinted by permission of Kate Navin, The Gersh Agency. For performance rights, contact Kate Navin (knavin@gershny.com).

THE FALLEN © 2010 by Yasmine Beverly Rana. Reprinted by permission of Susan Gurman, Susan Gurman Agency. For performance rights, contact Susan Gurman (susan@gurmanagency.com).

FEAR AND DESIRE © 2011 by Alana Ruben Free. Reprinted by permission of Alana Ruben Free. For performance rights, contact Alana Ruben Free (alana.free@gmail.com).

FIX ME, JESUS © 1994 by Helen Sneed. Reprinted by permission of Helen Sneed. For performance rights, contact Helen Sneed (hesneed@aol.com).

THE FUTURE IS NOT WHAT IT WAS © 2012 by Michael Rabe. Reprinted by permission of Michael Rabe. For performance rights, contact Michael Rabe (michael.c.rabe@gmail.com).

A GIRL'S GUIDE TO COFFEE © 2009 by Eric Coble. Reprinted by permission of Kate Navin, The Gersh Agency. For performance rights, contact Kate Navin (knavin@gershny.com).

HEADSTRONG © 2012 by Patrick Link. Reprinted by permission of Patrick Link. For performance rights, contact (patricklink1@gmail.com).

HIT-STORY © 2012 by Carter W. Lewis. Reprinted by permission of Susan Gurman, Susan Gurman Agency. For performance rights, contact Susan Gurman (susan@gurmanagency.com).

HIT THE WALL © 2013 by Ike Holter. Reprinted by permission of Val Day, ICM Partners. For performance rights, contact Val Day (vday@icmpartners.com).

HONKY © 2013 by Greg Kalleres. Reprinted by permission of Greg Kalleres. For performance rights, contact Ron Gwiazda, Abrams Artists Agency (ron.gwiazda@abramsartny.com).

HOUSEBREAKING © 2012 by Jakob Holder. Reprinted by permission of Jakob Holder, c/o The Gersh Agency. For performance rights, contact Dramatists Play Service, 440 Park Ave. S., New York, NY 10016 (www.dramatists.com) (212-683-8960).

HURRICANE © 2010 by Nilo Cruz. Reprinted by permission Peregrine Whittlesey. For performance rights, contact Peregrine Whittlesey (pwwagy@aol.com).

IMMEDIATE FAMILY © 2012 by Paul Oakley Stovall. Reprinted by permission of Susan Gurman, Susan Gurman Agency. For performance rights, contact Susan Gurman (susan@gurmanagency.com).

I THINK I LOVE YOU © 2012 by Sharon Goldner. Reprinted by permission of Sharon Goldner. For performance rights, contact Lawrence Harbison (LHarbison1@nyc. rr.com).

JESUS IN INDIA © 2012 by Lloyd Suh. Reprinted by permission of Beth Blickers, Abrams Artists Agency. For performance rights, contact Beth Blickers (beth. blickers@abramsartny.com).

JIHAD JONES AND THE KALASHNIVOV BABES © 2012 by Yussef El Guindi. Reprinted by permission of Morgan Jenness, Abrams Artists Agency. For performance rights, contact Morgan Jenness (morgan. jenness@abramsartny.com).

LIGHTNING FROM HEAVEN © 2013 by Scott Sickles. Reprinted by permission of Scott Sickles. For performance rights, contact Barbara Hogenson (bhogenson@aol.com).

LIVE BROADCAST © 2012 by John William Schiffbauer. Reprinted by permission of John William Schiffbauer, . For performance rights, contact Dramatists Play Service, 440 Park Ave. S., New York, NY 10016 (www. dramatists.com) (212-683-8960).

LUCY LOVES ME © 1987 by Migdalia Cruz. Reprinted by permission of Migdalia Cruz, c/o Peregrine Whittlesey. For performance rights, contact Peregrine Whittlesey (pwwagy@aol.com).

THE LYONS © 2012 by Nicky Silver. Reprinted by permission of John Buzzetti, William Morris Endeavor Entertainment. For performance rights, contact Dramatists Play Service, 440 Park Ave. S., New York, NY 10016 (www.dramatists.com) (212-683-8960).

THE MADRID © 2013 by Liz Flahive. Reprinted by permission of John Buzzetti, William Morris Endeavor Entertainment. For performance rights, contact Dramatists Play Service, 440 Park Ave. S., New York, NY 10016 (www.dramatists.com) (212-683-8960).

THE MAN UNDER © 2012 by Paul Bomba. Reprinted by permission of Paul Bomba. For performance rights, contact Paul Bomba (paul@paulbomba.com).

PIGEON © 2012 by Tommy Smith. Reprinted by permission of Tommy Smith, . For performance rights, contact Dramatists Play Service, 440 Park Ave. S., New York, NY 10016 (www.dramatists.com) (212-683-8960).

PILGRIMS MUSA AND SHERI IN THE NEW WORLD © 2012 by Yussef El Guindi. Reprinted by permission of Morgan Jenness, Abrams Artists Agency. For performance rights, contact Morgan Jenness (morgan.jenness@abramsartny.com).

PORT OUT, STARBOARD HOME © 2013 by Sheila Callaghan. Reprinted by permission of Corinne Hayoun, Creative Artists Agency. For performance rights, contact Corinne Hayoun (chayoun@caa.com).

PRINCES OF WACO © 2012 by Robert Askins. Reprinted by permission of Scott Chaloff, William Morris Endeavor Entertainment. For performance rights, contact Scott Chaloff (schaloff@wmeentertainment.com).

RADIANCE © 2012 by Cusi Cram. Reprinted by permission of Seth Glewen, The Gersh Agency. For performance rights, contact Seth Glewen (sglewen@gershny.com).

REALLY REALLY © 2012 by Paul Downs Colaizzo. Reprinted by permission of Val Day, ICM Partners. For performance rights, contact Dramatists Play Service, 440 Park Ave. S., New York, NY 10016 (www.dramatists.com) (212-683-8960).

SEED © 2013 by Radha Blank. Reprinted by permission of Kate Navin, The Gersh Agency. For performance rights, contact Kate Navin (knavin@gershny.com).

SLOWGIRL © 2012 by Greg Pierce. Reprinted by permission of Scott Chaloff, William Morris Endeavor Entertainment. For performance rights, contact Dramatists Play Service, 440 Park Ave. S., New York, NY 10016 (www.dramatists.com) (212-683-8960).

SOFT REVOLUTION: SHAFANA AND AUNT SARRINAH © 2013 by Alana Valentine. Reprinted by permission of Peregrine Whittlesey. For performance rights, contact Peregrine Whittlesey (pwwagy@aol.com).

TEN CHIMNEYS © 2012 by Jeffrey Hatcher. Reprinted by permission of Jack Tantleff, Paradigm. For performance rights, contact Dramatists Play Service, 440 Park Ave. S., New York, NY 10016 (www.dramatists.com) (212-683-8960).

TERESA'S ECSTACY © 2012 by Begonya Plaza. Reprinted by permission of Begonya Plaza. For performance rights, contact Broadway Play Publishing, 212-772-8334, www.broadwayplaypubl.com

THIS IS FICTION © 2012 by Megan Hart. Reprinted by permission of Megan Hart. For performance rights, contact Megan Hart (meganhart@gmail.com).

THE TIGER AMONG US © 2012 by Lauren Yee. Reprinted by permission of Antje Oegel, AO International. For performance rights, contact Antje Oegel (aoegel@aoegelinternational.com).

TIME IN KAFKA © 2012 by Len Jenkin. Reprinted by permission of Morgan Jenness, Abrams Artists Agency. For performance rights, contact Broadway Play Publishing, 212-772-8334, www.broadwayplaypubl.com

THE VANDAL © 2013 by Hamish Linklater. Reprinted by permission of Val Day, ICM Partners. For performance rights, contact Dramatists Play Service, 440 Park Ave. S., New York, NY 10016 (www.dramatists.com) (212-683-8960).

VANYA AND SONIA AND MASHA AND SPIKE © 2013 by Christopher Durang. Reprinted by permission of Christopher Durang, c/o, ICM Partners. For performance rights, contact Dramatists Play Service, 440 Park Ave. S., New York, NY 10016 (www.dramatists.com) (212-683-8960).

VENUS IN FUR © 2012 by David Ives. Reprinted by permission of Peter Hagan, Abrams Artists Agency. For performance rights, contact Dramatists Play Service, 440 Park Ave. S., New York, NY 10016 (www.dramatists.com) (212-683-8960).